To Marilyn,

Your Life's Echo

with best wishes
for a successfull
feature!

Your Life's Echo

"How to get ahead faster and easier than you ever imagined in your business and personal life"

Oddmund Berger

LIFESUCCESS PUBLISHING, LLC
8900 E Pinnacle Peak Road, Suite D240
Scottsdale, AZ 85255

Telephone:	800.473.7134
Fax:	480.661.1014
E-mail:	admin@lifesuccesspublishing.com
ISBN:	978-159930-119-8
Cover:	Erick Sellers & LifeSuccess Publishing
Layout:	Erick Sellers & LifeSuccess Publishing

COMPANIES, ORGANIZATIONS, INSTITUTIONS, AND INDUSTRY PUBLICATIONS: Quantity discounts are available on bulk purchases of this book for reselling, educational purposes, subscription incentives, gifts, sponsorship, or fundraising. Special books or book excerpts can also be created to fit specific needs such as private labeling with your logo on the cover and a message from a VIP printed inside. For more information please contact our Special Sales Department at LifeSuccess Publishing.

Dedication

I would like to dedicate this book to my wife, Angelika, the best companion, friend and life partner I could ever imagine. I thank her for her support during this project, and for her wisdom and insights that added so much. This book will launch on almost the same day as our 5th anniversary, and I can say that it has been the most wonderful five years of my life.

I would also like to acknowledge the best possible parents a man could ever have, Wenche and Odd, who are now only a couple of years away from their fiftieth anniversary. I am truly fortunate to have their encouragement and support for whatever I do. This dedication would not be complete without my sister Nina and her children, Kristin and Thomas. She has always supported me and is a great inspiration to me.

My wife's family has also been a large support to both our endeavors, and I also consider myself very fortunate to be included in their midst. I would also offer a special thanks to Angelika's mother Doris and her late father Klaus, who left us much too early and just before this book came out. Angelika's family includes Thomas and Andrea with Lara; Felix and Ulrike with Hannah and Luise; and sister Conny and husband Horst with Marcel and Jana. Thank you all for your support.

Acknowledgements

One of the most important influences in my life has been Bob Proctor, my friend and mentor. Aside from being a wonderfully generous human being, he has taught me more in the last three years than I had learned in the last four decades, both professionally as well as personally. He provided the best material in the world for me to learn from and has now given me the chance to teach it to others. For this, the words "thank you" seem inadequate. I only hope I can pass along Bob's wisdom to those who are seeking as I once was.

I would also like to thank my friends and business partners Henning and Liv Hverven, for the combination of friendship, inspiration and personal fulfillment as we have built our businesses together. I would also offer my gratitude to Wolfgang Sonnenburg, my friend and mentor, for all our good conversations and all the great advice I received in developing myself and my businesses.

I thank Ingemar and Betty Fredriksson, William Todd, and Reid Nelson for the help and inspiration they gave me while I was building my first business.

I would like to acknowledge Paul Martinelli, President of LifeSuccess Consulting, for his great inspiration and leadership, as well as the board and management of LifeSuccess productions: Mark Meyerdirk, Gina Hayden, Gerry Robert, Hugh Nicholson along with their teams. I would also like to thank the entire team at LifeSuccess Publishing for making this book a reality. I would like to direct a special thanks to Dee Burks for her invaluable contribution to the development of the book, and to Kandi Miller for managing the entire project.

For many years I have been surrounded by great friends who have positively influenced my life. They include Jan Andersson, Atle Hansen, Jon Pettersen, Nils Sundling, Egil Bråthe, Michael Gabrielsson, and Patty and Bert Wohl with family. Thank you for being my friends and inspiring me in a multitude of different ways. I thank Bjørn Elvestad for his inspiration and valuable insights to the application of the book, and I also thank Terje Sand, my former teacher at Oslo Business School, for his teachings that inspired me to a career in sales and marketing. I would like to thank my friend Geir Monge for his part in inspiring me to become an entrepreneur and start my own business. I would also like to thank Seija Wolauz for the contribution to the title of the book and her inspiration to me.

Last, but certainly not least, I would like to thank my extended family, friends, current and former leaders and other colleagues, business partners, teachers, coaches, students, and customers for the contribution each and every one of them made to the person I am today. They are the inspiration for this book and have all been instrumental in teaching me the natural law that is so often called "the law of laws," the Law of Cause and Effect, which is the basis for this book - *Your Life's Echo*.

Foreword

Several years ago I had the privilege of meeting a gentleman who has since become a good friend of mine. We share a passion for study. Oddmund Berger has been a serious student of human potential for a couple of decades and possesses incredible insight into what it takes to move from the ordinary to the extraordinary.

As Napoleon Hill states, "No more effort is required to aim high in life, to demand abundance and prosperity than is required to accept misery and poverty."

.In our fast-paced and ever-changing world, success is a highly sought-after commodity. But, what's impressive is that people are looking beyond the superficial and taking a holistic approach to life in wanting not only success, but balance in their personal lives and relationships.

Many of the high chargers, those people who really make it happen in a big way, would be hard-pressed to articulate why or how they've accomplished so much in their lives. In Your Life's Echo, Oddmund Berger has removed the mystery and illustrates the concepts that these successful individuals have integrated into their lives. It IS possible to have both success and balance as you move through life.

This book carries practical advice and examples that can be used by the business leader and athlete alike. Regardless of what set of circumstances has gotten you to where you are today, realize that you have the ability to change the way you think and change the way you live … starting now. There's nothing complicated about it. All it takes is a decision, right now, today.

I once heard it said that the late President John F. Kennedy had his speeches written so that a 5th grader could understand them. Over the years, this technique has proven very successful in my teachings and Oddmund has adopted a similar style in his writing. He has the unique ability to effectively communicate complex ideas in a very straight-forward way that speaks directly to audiences worldwide.

There are no shortcuts to success, but quantum leaps can be experienced and enjoyed through the transference of information and experience. Your Life's Echo is rich in wisdom and experience that will help any person BE more, DO more or HAVE more.

Life isn't a practice run. For all we know, we only get one bite at the apple and to my knowledge, nobody has a contract to live forever. We have a choice … we can continue on autopilot as we did the day before or we can choose to heighten our awareness of our potential and go for what we truly want!

Open your mind and your heart and be ready to take in all this book has to teach. You can and will be transformed – I guarantee it.

– Bob Proctor
Bestselling author of *You Were Born Rich*

Table of Contents

Introduction

The book you hold in your hands is a personal dream of mine and a lifetime accumulation of knowledge. As you journey through this information, I want to encourage you to open your mind and free yourself from your present and past circumstances and results.

If you feel successful and on your way forward in life, my hope is that this book will give you added awareness as to why you have achieved your success in different areas, whether within your profession, sports, relationships and family or other areas, and also provide insight to allow you to grow more and teach others what you have learned. Most successful people are not aware of why they have become so successful, and will therefore have problems articulating or teaching others so that they can take advantage of their experiences.

Should you, on the other hand, feel a little "stuck" in life, your career, or your business, or maybe know someone in that situation, I want to share with you that there is hope for you or that person to take charge of your lives, regardless of where you are and what background you come from.

Should you be of the opinion, "I like my life just the way it is," you will find information in these pages indicating why this isn't necessarily a beneficial attitude to have. I will explain that nothing in this universe stands still, meaning we are either moving forward in life or backward, and the direction you take is a conscious choice. I will discuss the idea of your life's "Echo" and what it tells you. An echo is a direct reflection of what you produce. Your life echo is the results you are achieving through your current actions and behaviors.

I believe it was Emerson who said The Law of Cause and Effect is "the Law of Laws," and that, "If you put a little bit in, you get a little bit out, but if you put a whole lot in, you'll get a whole lot out." Dr. Wernher Von Braun, called the father of the modern space program by many, indicated that, "The natural laws of this universe are so precise that we have no difficulty building a space ship, sending people to the moon and we can time the landing with the precision of a fraction of a second." Most people are not aware of these forces or are subconsciously using them to their disadvantage. I have found that if you make the decision to have these natural forces work for you, you have a much better chance to advance your personal life as well as your professional life, your team, organization or your business.

If you are a corporate CEO or executive, I would challenge you to view these pages as the transformational edge you have been looking for in your business. The ability to lead is grounded in the fact that workers today must be personally fulfilled in order to be loyal and productive for your company. Gone are the days of hiring a worker with the expectation that they will be with you for thirty plus years and retire. Workers today want more personal freedom and fulfillment. The executive who realizes that fact will keep the best workers in their chosen field and continue to add value for their stockholders. I believe that to attract the best employees today requires different offerings. Whereas before many leaders would argue that the frame would be more important than the freedom under which the employees would work, I believe we are now moving in the opposite direction.

In years past, CEOs of companies would strive to create a corporate culture where the employees' patriotism meant total dedication and loyalty, and that the employees' only source of income would be from the company. I believe the modern employee wants to provide service in several ways to earn their income from multiple sources, while at the same time choosing to work for satisfaction in the company.

> *Workers today want more personal freedom and fulfillment.*

Employees want to do what they love. They want to be "on purpose" working for your organization and dedicated to your vision. They are becoming increasingly aware that no job is "secure," and that each and every person will be compensated in direct relation to the need for what they do, their ability to do it, and the difficulty of replacing them. Employees will be as loyal to the company as the company is to them. I have found this to be as true for a normal business, a football or soccer team when attracting and keeping the right players and administrative staff, as well as voluntary organizations.

This information, when applied correctly, is beneficial and many times life changing to people at any level in their development who want to improve their results in different areas of their personal life or within their profession or business. When suggesting this, I am of course fully aware of and respect the necessary balance you need to keep as far as obligations and respect to your family's situation. However, there are in most, if not all, situations ways to create and design the life you want while keeping family relations well-balanced.

No matter how your life has been up until now, I want you to know that you can improve it, even change it altogether if that is your wish. You can improve your physical health, get that promotion you wanted, start that business you've always dreamed about, find that lifelong mate you've hoped for, or turn your yearly salary into your monthly salary. How? By taking control and expanding your thinking. This expansion includes all areas of life, not just financial, but also physical health, family, friendships and relationships, career, education, and personal development, all areas in life that have meaning to you.

This is not just another book about positive thought, but a book to show you how your present and past results are nothing but the manifestation of how you have been thinking up until now, and that those results can be changed. How many times have you met a person who had a negative outlook on life? Nothing ever goes their way; they complain and are unpleasant to be around. Their attitude attracts more unpleasant events into their lives, and they continue on a downward spiral. It is logical that if negative thoughts can have that kind of powerful impact on a person's life, then positive thoughts combined with action can have an equally powerful impact.

No matter your business or corporate position, there is useful information to be gleaned from these pages and passed on to those whom you are acquainted with, those who work for you, and even to those you go home to everyday. The question you must ask yourself is do you want your business and personal life to be on the cutting edge of this transformational change, or left behind? If you desire the best for your family and yourself, then the ideas presented here can help.

> *Have you ever thought about what you want from life?*

Within these pages, we'll talk about what you really want.
Have you ever thought about what you want from life? I mean
seriously thought about it? We'll discuss in detail how to determine
your life's purpose and what you envision in your future. We'll
also have an in-depth discussion of how you arrived at this point
in your life. How have you been preconditioned to accept limiting
beliefs, and what steps you must take to break free of those
ingrained thought patterns?

> ## *Just because you can't hear it,*
> ## *doesn't mean it's not there.*

You may feel that this book challenges your beliefs, your
comfort zone, and the way you were raised to think. Most of us
were taught what to think rather than how to think while growing
up, and this lead us to certain ideas about how we view the world.
I encourage you to keep an open mind while reading. As we
sometimes say in Norway, "There is more between heaven and
earth than you can see with your eyes only."

Let me ask you: Do you hear opera or classical music
right now? If not, you know there is opera or classic music where
you are right now, don't you? Just because you can't hear it,
doesn't mean it's not there. You are just not "tuned in" on the right
frequency. If you placed a small radio close to you and tuned into
the right station, I am sure you would find the music. Just because
we don't see or hear the evidence immediately in our awareness,

that's no proof that it doesn't exist. You see, all there ever was, or ever will be, is one-hundred percent present at all times. The way to communicate over internet was always there; we were just not aware of it. The way to fly an airplane was always there; we were just not aware of it until the Wright brothers gave us the information. Awareness comes from understanding, which in turn comes from studying. So please keep an open mind, and I believe you will benefit greatly when understanding the information provided in this book.

I came from a background where the term "energy" to me meant something that comes out of the wall when plugging in the PC. However, I now know that energy is all around us, and we can choose to harness that energy to create the outcomes we choose. Through being open- minded and studious of positive philosophies, I discovered there is more to life than I previously realized. As illustrated above, "The absence of evidence is not the evidence of absence."

Unfortunately, we are all raised to believe certain things about ourselves and our potential. Though most of us recognize we can change, we don't. Why? Knowing something doesn't mean we apply it, and so our lives pass one day after the next and nothing improves. We have the ability to choose our lives and our success, but we invariably spend much of our time with needless worries about things such as:

"I won't be able to spend enough time with my children."

"I don't know enough about business to start one of my own."

"I'm too afraid of rejection to get involved in a relationship."

"I don't have the money to invest."

"I don't have the time to spare."

"I'm not educated enough to learn about new ideas."

I'll show you the reality that none of these worries are valid. The only person holding you back from a lifestyle of abundance is you.

Many of us fear risk, yet it is a natural part of our existence. You must not let fear of the past, uncertainty in the present, or worries about the future stop you from seeking the life you were meant to live, a life that is in line with your true purpose.

The ideas of personal responsibility and accountability will help you take ownership of your choices and reject the victim syndrome that so many people fall into. In order to be different, you must think differently. This involves active choices that you can make everyday to change your thoughts and therefore, your life.

Indeed, you have what it takes to be successful; we all do. However, few have the persistence to seek out the opportunities life has for them. We become comfortable and complacent, and are reluctant to embrace change even when we desperately need to. By comparing ourselves to others and believing we are simply average, we limit our potential.

Anything you ever want to accomplish begins with a decision to do it, and I encourage you to accept the ideas presented here as the first of many stepping stones to a new and better life, a life of insight where you can design the abundant lifestyle you really want to live, the job or sports career you want to have, or the business you want to create regardless of circumstances, conditions, or environment.

– Oddmund Berger

Chapter One

The Dream

Chapter One

The Dream

"Cherish your visions and your dreams, as they are the children of your soul, the blueprints of your ultimate achievements."

— Napoleon Hill

No one sets out in life to fail. As humans it is our nature to strive for more, desire more and dream of all the possibilities the future holds. If you ask any five-year-old, they can articulate a list of dreams they already have for their life, which might include their future occupation, but will almost always include how they will feel. They want to be happy.

As we all grow into adulthood, our idea of happiness takes the form of creating a specific lifestyle. We want an education, a good job, a family. Most people work very hard to achieve these things and many actually attain them, yet are unhappy. They have discovered the same problem that I experienced after years as an Executive Vice President: It isn't things, the prestige of a title, or position that make you happy. Happiness is something that comes from within.

It is my belief that if you don't like the situation you are in, or heading toward, you should take action to change things. I am also of the opinion that "you don't need to be sick to become better," meaning that you can choose a better life even though at the time, your life is satisfactory. I have found that to be true for physical health as well as for any other part in life; you can always improve. At the time I decided to change my life, I was happy and my physical health was excellent. I had a good job in top management at a large corporation, and had experienced numerous successes in my career. I liked my boss and my work colleagues. My finances were good; I had friends around me and a wonderful family at home in Norway that supported me in all my endeavors.

> *Happiness is something that comes from within.*

After having achieved so many of my goals and desires, my life still felt a little out of balance. My life echo wasn't particularly satisfying, and I always seemed too tired to invest as much time as I wanted into my family and other relationships.

I couldn't see myself continuing to work sixty to eighty hours
a week and traveling one- hundred and fifty days per year for
the next thirty years in order to retire tired and exhausted at age
sixty-five. I realized that what I really wanted and needed was a
lifestyle that allowed me to refocus, rebalance, and achieve the
freedom to pursue my own individual dream of happiness. I heard
Bob Proctor once say, "In order to change your life, you've got to
change your life." He was right. It is a sad fact today that many
people start worrying on Sunday afternoon that another work week
is approaching. They then spend much of the time commuting to
work Monday morning thinking about the work environment they
hate, a manager they can't understand and a job that's not fulfilling,
all the while knowing their biggest fear is getting fired! As
mentioned, I really did like my job. My problem was that it took
too much out of me. In order to change my life, I had to make the
decision and then begin a journey of discovery to make it happen.
You can do the same. The ability to live the life of your dreams is
not being withheld from you by any person or any obstacle. No
one stands in your way, no one but you.

If Money Was No Object

Freedom for many people is a powerful concept and, for
most, intimately entwined with their finances. While your life is
not all about money, it is a large concern for many people. They
want freedom with respect to work and a possibility to engage in a
job that is in harmony with their purpose without having to worry
about bills. The daily grind of living a life is not exactly what they

imagined. However, they have no idea how to go about setting into motion a process to change and rebalance their lives. Feeling trapped, they move through each day accepting their fate and giving in to emotional helplessness.

> ## *No one stands in your way, no one but you.*

I will ask you, for a moment, to set aside the pressure of finances, job performance, work environment for just a moment and think about how your life would be if:

- Money was no object.

- You could choose where to spend your time.

- You knew you couldn't fail.

Imagine how your life would look and what you would do differently. Would you be working as much or even have the same job? Would you pay more attention to the signs and symptoms of unease in your work environment? Would you still work for others, building their dreams, or would you start your own business? Would you share more of your life with family and friends? Would you travel and see the world?

Understand that this exercise is not about anyone quitting their job. This is about gaining the freedom to live a lifestyle that gives you what you want. If you love your current occupation, then you only need to expand your lifestyle to achieve more balance and look for other opportunities that enhance your existing skills. If you want your employees to be challenged and inspired by their jobs, you must provide opportunities for them to balance their lives as well.

It is a fact that employees spend an average of less than five years at a job before switching employers. Given the opportunity, many people will take a lower paying job that is fulfilling over a high pressure job that is not. Life balance is becoming increasingly important for the majority of workers. Without the persistent financial pressures, many would seek fulfillment in a job they like rather than stress in a job they don't like. As an employer, it gets more expensive every day to ignore the fact that employees need balance.

A good example of this balance is a friend from my small hometown of 25,000 people. My friend has been a successful hairdresser for years and loves his work. When you think of the lifestyle of most hairdressers, it is not an abundant one. Many merely trade their time for money for most of their lives, just managing to keep the bills paid, and then retire early worn out. This man has developed his skill into a business with several salons and has also added successful investments in real estate. He lives a very different lifestyle than most other hairdressers, enjoying both time and monetary freedom. He is also an example to those who work with him and for him of the lifestyle they can achieve as well.

I use this example to point out that you don't have to be an Executive Vice President or born into wealth to achieve a lifestyle of freedom. You can be a hairdresser, doctor, nurse, or mechanic, it doesn't matter. By starting with what you have and where you are right now in your life, you can set upon the path to great things, but only if you can imagine it.

The Mindset of Expansion

I heard my business partner Paul Martinelli, President of LifeSuccess Consulting, once say, "Nobody's going to die your death, so why on earth should you allow someone else to live your life?" You can never be in line with your purpose if you feel you must always "please" other people. We build certain paradigms throughout life and are conditioned by genetics and environment. We are a product of the authorities or people we surround ourselves with. If you know someone whose life echo is unsatisfying or displeases them, then the good news is that those paradigms can be changed and they can take control of their lives.

> *You can never be in line with your purpose if you feel you must always "please" other people.*

Each person has an idea of what the perfect lifestyle would be. For some, this may be living in a certain location or type of home. Others may want more time to spend with children, parents and friends. Some may also view it as the opportunity to share with others or build a business. Think about what your perfect lifestyle would be. Get specific and dream big. What would you want if neither money nor time was a problem, and you knew you couldn't fail?

There are those individuals that you see on television and in the course of daily living that seem to already be living the lifestyle you would love to have. Have you ever caught yourself thinking, "Must be nice," or dismissing them as lucky or born into the right family? We all can get caught up in this mindset, but the difference between you and them is not in what they have or how they live. It is in how they *think*. They have cultivated a mindset of expansion, and this enables them to bring abundance into their lives with seemingly little effort.

You may instantly reject the idea that someone can *think* abundance into their lives as ridiculous. I understand that hesitation, but I would also ask how many people live their lives thinking poor? How many friends or coworkers do you know who are convinced they will never rise above their present circumstances, no matter how hard they try, and dismiss any attempt to do so as unrealistic? It is only logical to understand that if thinking poor can have that kind of negative impact on a person's life, then thinking wealthy must also have the same impact, but in a positive way. You can achieve if only you can dream! Some may wonder, "If the mindset of expansion can offer so much, why don't more people use it?"

> ## *You can achieve if only you can dream!*

Comb. With 3 How To

Many individuals live their lives as though the things they want have a finite source. This creates a mindset of scarcity, lack, and limitation, as in, "There is only so much to go around and the odds of me getting my share are small. Therefore, I have to work hard and get what I can." This mindset occurs because the ideas of scarcity have been ingrained into our thought process over time. These are ideas such as the following:

- You can't get a decent job without the right education.

- Don't ask for too much.

- You shouldn't aim too high up the corporate ladder or you'll be disappointed.

- You can't make mistakes and get ahead.

- It's better to be safe than sorry.

- You can't expect to be successful with no experience.

- Don't expect miracles.

Some of these concepts, sayings, and ideas are so ingrained that we don't even realize we think them, yet they all encourage a mindset of scarcity. Scarcity breeds fear, and it is shocking how many people choose to live their lives fearing what tomorrow will bring, what they don't know, and what they can't change.

If you have done your best to run a business and have tried everything you know to be successful, you have probably encountered this mindset. It is important to understand as a business leader that by helping the individual, you also help the company. We are the collection of our experiences, and by encouraging those around you to be the best that they can be, you encourage them to produce the best possible results for the company. So when I present ideas that seem to only help the person, you must realize that better people make a better company.

In Scandinavia there is even a "culture" for envying people who have been successful. People who have been successful in business, for example, are often looked upon by the masses with suspicion, as if they must have done something criminal to achieve that success, or that they are clearly operating in the "grey zone." If you, however, won a few million in the lottery or are a sports or pop star, then success seems more acceptable. However, if you go bankrupt in Scandinavia, people often say, "I could have told him that wouldn't work." In this case, I prefer the American attitude. It seems to me that Americans appreciate failure and setbacks as useful experiences and would rather say, "Well done, at least you tried. Better luck next time."

While some seem locked in their misery complaining of what they don't have, the mindset of expansion does just the opposite. It acknowledges that there is unlimited abundance in the universe and that by growing and expanding ideas, dreams, and thoughts, that abundance becomes very real. There is no need to hoard your ideas or hide your goals. In a mindset of expansion, sharing your vision and dreams only expands them. Once you understand that there is no finite limit to what you want to achieve, you will revel in abundance.

> *As my good friend Bob Proctor says, "If you have a problem, the person you need to talk with is always available; you just have to look in the mirror."*

Knowing and Doing

I have another friend who contacted me a short time ago. She felt stuck in her sales-related business. As I listened to her talk, she had completely focused her mind on the previous lack of results and spent all of her time trying desperately to change those results. She constantly worried about when the change would occur. What she really needed to change was her own mindset. She was so focused on her fears that she created even more fear and negativity. She then made it worse by seeking "comfort" and taking advice from others who were also stuck and fearful. There is an old saying that "Misery loves company." By surrounding herself with others who were equally worried and fearful, she validated and perpetuated those fears, virtually blocking any attempt at positive results. As my good friend Bob Proctor says, "If you have a problem, the person you need to talk with is always available; you just have to look in the mirror."

Many of us know what to do. We want our time to be our own and to live in freedom. We know we should look for opportunities, take the most promising ones and move forward. If we want different results in our lives, we focus on change. The problem is that we do not change ourselves or our mindset. We focus on the negative by giving in to fear, fear that we will fail, and so it becomes self-fulfilling. It is important to understand that which you think about, you will become. It is a conscious decision to accept the mindset of expansion, and it takes effort. If it were easy, every business would try it. Only those business leaders who understand the current transformation occurring within their employee base will benefit, and those employees will benefit as well by achieving rewarding abundant lives.

This applies to all areas of life in which one wishes to experience abundance, whether it is career, family, health, or finances. Think for a moment of all the detrimental health habits people have. Some smoke, drink to excess, and refuse to exercise. It is no secret that these choices are bad for good health, yet many refuse to change. They cling strongly to those habits and associate with those who have similar habits, further validating their poor choices. The power to change any aspect of your life is completely within your control, but only if you change your thoughts. This could also mean changing your associations, but it is necessary if you truly want to live an abundant life. In order to transform your life and echo your true self, you must first transform the mind.

We Are All the Same

I have traveled the world and worked in many countries with people from many different places. My experience has been that when we take away group habits, what we call "culture," we are all essentially alike. We need and want a balanced lifestyle to feel happy, healthy and to have a high quality of life. It matters not that we speak different languages, have different beliefs, or pursue different goals. It matters not whether we are Chairman of the Board or work in a factory. Our minds still work in exactly the same fashion. We all have intellectual faculties that make us completely different than any other animal, yet we posses these same skills across all cultures and races. They are uniquely human.

> *The five senses are limited to telling and showing us what already "is."*

We are all born with five senses: sight, taste, touch, hearing, and smell. By the age of five, most children have a complete understanding of their ability to use their five senses to understand the world and environment around them. The five senses are limited to telling and showing us what already "is". They have no power to create or transform.

Intellectual faculties do have the power to create and transform. They are present in each one of us, and each identifies a powerful area of thought that we can use to change our thoughts and transform our lives.

The six intellectual faculties are

- Reasoning (both Deductive and Inductive)

- Intuition

- Will

- Perception

- Imagination

- Memory

In order for us to utilize our mind and provide each of us with the life echo of our dreams, we must develop these faculties which are much like mental muscles. It is also imperative to understand that these faculties are always at work. However, they may be weak or strong, depending on how much you use them. It may be helpful to your understanding to compare these mental muscles to the physical muscles in your body. If you exercise your muscles consistently and provide them with proper nutrition and rest, they will grow and expand. However, if you stop the consistent exercise and ignore their needs, your muscles will atrophy. The six intellectual faculties operate in the same way. Your ability to have the life of your dreams starts with your thoughts. Being able to *think wealthy* is proportional to the development, integration, and strength of these six faculties which, when exercised, expand infinitely. We will discuss each of these faculties separately to be sure you grasp the importance and function of each one.

> *Your ability to have the life of your dreams starts with your thoughts.*

Reasoning

Archibald McLeisch is a Pulitzer Prize-winning playwright. In his play *The Secret of Freedom*, a character says, "The only thing about a man that is a man is his mind. Everything else can be found in a pig or a horse." The human mind is the one thing that separates us from the rest of the creatures on earth.

The highest faculty of our minds is our ability to reason. Reasoning is our ability to make sense of events in our world. Deductive Reasoning is our default thought process that insures that we will continue to be a product of our environment. Your deductive reasoning relies on your current understanding and conditioning at the subconscious level for guidance. This is harmful if you lack the results you desire because, as we will show you with the Stickperson concept in the next chapter, your results are merely the outflow of your previous thought patterns and "truths" you have learned over time.

When you are deductively reasoning, you will quickly reject anything that doesn't match your current understanding or paradigms. A paradigm is a multitude of habits or fixed ideas in your subconscious mind. This guarantees that you will continue to act on ideas that keep that paradigm in place, and are likely to reject an idea that would move your life, career, or wealth forward. You will also likely stay in your comfort zone when you are being deductive. Your attitudes will be created by your surrounding environment rather than creating the environment that surrounds you. You are purely deductive when your environment creates you, and you are being inductive when you create your own environment.

Inductive Reasoning (True Thinking) occurs when we use our intuition, perception, will, imagination, and memory to analyze new ideas and then create and support the picture of what we want to see manifest with new thought patterns.

Have you ever come home to your parents, your spouse, or told a friend about some new idea that you would like to put into action - that you want to become a leader and apply for a leadership position in your company, or travel the world with a back pack, or start a new business or some other "crazy" idea? Were they all immediately supportive? Or did they instead start playing "the devil's advocate" with you? We are in many ways programmed from the early days of our lives to look for what's wrong with things and ideas, rather than to first look for what's good.

In Norway, where I grew up, one of the first games I was introduced to was a page with two seemingly identical pictures. Above the pictures were the instructions, "Find five mistakes in one of the pictures." Our quest for seeking out the problems or issues with a situation starts very young; it progresses further when we have experienced teachers in school correcting mistakes. On my tests it usually said, for example, "Three mistakes." Seldom does a test read "ninety-seven correct." We get this in the business world as well. Evaluating employees on what they do wrong, rather than what they do right, as many employers still do, provides consistently negative feedback. This traditional mindset of correction rather than encouragement is quickly disappearing. There are too many opportunities for good employees with companies that are more forward thinking. Why would you run the risk of forcing them to leave?

While serving in the military, our sergeant found mistakes with everything from my uniform to the way I shaved or how I walked. This continued in my work environment and is probably prevalent in yours, as well. How often do you tell employees or coworkers that you appreciate all they do right? Instead, most of us focus on the missed sales quota, botched report, or lack of cooperation on a certain project. No wonder we are afraid of making mistakes.

When we come across an opportunity to start a new
business or some other idea we find attractive to include in our
lives, what do we normally do? We ask some person around us that
we respect for their opinion: "What do you think?" The problem,
however, is that they normally don't think. Earl Nightingale once
stated, "If the average person said what they were thinking, they
would be speechless." Just observe people around you. Most move
through their daily lives on autopilot, mistaking mental activity for
thinking. There is very little new thinking going on.

> *Earl Nightingale once stated, "If*
> *the average person said what they*
> *were thinking, they would*
> *be speechless."*

When you come upon a new idea, let's say that you
would like to become a consultant and a public speaker but have
never tried it, you will normally ask what other people think. It
is interesting that we have a tendency to ask authorities around
us, people that we have respect for as a person and for their
competencies in other areas, what they think of this new idea of
becoming a public speaker. They don't have competence in the
area of public speaking, yet we take their opinions to heart.

Think of it in another way: if you wanted to learn to
fly an airplane, would you ask a dentist for advice on how to
fly? Probably not. What's even more amazing is how strong the

opinions of these people are that are being asked about things that they know very little about. The mistake we make is that we listen to this well- intended advice from kind people who don't know what they are talking about, and then let that advice steer our thinking and decision making.

The rule I follow is this: If you allow other people to make your decisions, you better be sure that they have one-hundred percent phenomenal results in all areas of life because you will be following the same path. Collect information with your five senses and do your research, but when it comes to making a decision, trust yourself; don't ask others. As Napoleon Hill states in his book *Think and Grow Rich*, "Opinions are the cheapest commodities on earth." Yet people offer them in abundance, often out of a flawed sense of kindness or trying to "save you" from making mistakes. Unfortunately, often they are also stealing your dream and holding you from a rich and fulfilling life.

My wife, Angelika, has had former careers as a server in a restaurant, a kindergarten assistant, and also spent eight years as a secretary. Several years ago, she told some of her closest friends that she intended to start her own business. The response was difficult to handle. They said things such as, "This will definitely not fit your personality; you are much too nice," and, "This is not meant for you; you don't know anything about how a business works." These were just two of many comments which would have made other people pull back and surrender their dream. If she had been thinking only deductively, she would probably still be a secretary somewhere and we would never have met. Thanks to her unconscious competence at the time (she was not consciously aware of how she was thinking) in thinking inductively, she followed her dream and her heart and started what has become one of the most successful businesses in the world in her industry. She took the risk and saw her former yearly income as a secretary turn into her new monthly income.

> *When the still small voice answers, you must act immediately.*

Intuition

Often referred to as our "sixth sense," our intuition is our ability to connect with another individual without even knowing or speaking to them. When we meet someone who immediately makes us feel good or positive, that person projects a positive energy and our intuition senses it. When we meet someone who makes us feel negative or scared, our intuition immediately warns us of the negativity. Napoleon Hill's *Think and Grow Rich* explains that when you demand a definite plan from your mind for abundance, be on alert because it will and must answer you, but it will do so through *inspired thought,* or the sixth sense. When the still small voice answers, you must act immediately. Failure to do so will be fatal to success. Developing your intuition to tune in to the highest level of those around you allows you to see through

all the noise of conversation, and immediately understand the
essence of who they are and what they are about. My best advice
to you for exercising this mental muscle is to trust it, then act on it
immediately.

Some years ago I lived and worked from Stockholm,
Sweden. My little hometown in Norway was a six or seven hour
drive away. Since I enjoy driving while thinking or studying by
listening to CDs, I decided to take the car to visit my parents and
friends for a few days while my wife was in Germany. Around
7:30 on a Saturday evening, I was halfway through the trip and
stopped at a restaurant to eat. As I finished my meal, my mobile
phone rang and my wife was on the other end. I sat down and
we talked for about thirty minutes before I continued my journey
toward Norway. Angelika said that she "just felt like calling." We
speak everyday, no matter where we are in the world, but seldom
agree on a specific time to call; we just call when it feels right.
However, on this day we had it agreed to talk when I arrived, so
it was quite out of the ordinary. An hour or so later it had grown
dark as I approached the Norwegian border. I suddenly saw many
lights as I came through the woods. There were police cars, the fire
brigade and ambulances. A police man stopped me as the fourth car
in line. I asked what happened and if I could be of any help, but he
thanked me and said it was too late. Two cars traveling right after
each other had collided with a couple of moose as these enormous
animals tried to cross the road in the dark. Due to the high speed
of the cars, the drivers had no chance to avoid the animals. From

the silent ambulances driving away, I understood that some people had lost their lives that evening. I asked the policeman when it happened and he looked at his watch. "It must be quite exactly thirty minutes ago," based upon what the witnesses had told him who were first on scene. A cold chill sneaked down my back as I realized that I could be thankful that although we had agreed to talk when I arrived, Angelika followed her intuition that evening, that inner voice that told her to give me a call anyway. If she hadn't called and I hadn't sat down to talk with her for thirty minutes, I could have been in one of those cars.

Malcolm Gladwell is the best-selling author of *The Tipping Point* and *Blink: The Power of Thinking without Thinking.* In the latter he discusses a term he calls "thin-slicing," which is the phenomenon of taking the smallest amount of information possible and using it to make a judgment or decision. He illustrates, through numerous real-world examples and scientific research, that when you properly learn to "thin slice" in the area of your business, career, personal, or financial life, your quick judgments and analyses are often more insightful and better than those made with *more information.* Thin-slicing relies heavily on the skill of intuition and can work for you or against you depending on which paradigms are ruling your subconscious.

> *Perception is what we use to create meaning from events or experiences in our life.*

Perception

Perception is what we use to create meaning from events or experiences in our life. We interpret these based on past events and conditioning. An important concept to understand with perception is that everything is relative. The Universal Law of Relativity states that nothing has meaning, or is good or bad, big or small, cheap or expensive until we make it so. Thus, each person will have a different perception or interpretation of exactly the same event or object.

Think about money for example: What is $20,000? Some may say that $20,000 is a great deal of money, while others think that $20,000 is a trivial amount. The truth is that $20,000 just "is." Perception can have both very positive and very negative effects. For example, if a company has poor financial results one year and only offers employees a one-percent raise, one employee may see it as a very positive event since he knew the company had been doing poorly and didn't expect any raise at all. His attitude will be positive and he will continue to perform in an upbeat and efficient manner. However, another employee may see the same one-percent raise as a slap in the face and complain about management and how unfairly they treat workers. This employee's attitude will plummet, and his negativity will manifest itself in poor performance.

We are, to a large extent, a product of other people's habitual way of thinking. If your parents and other authorities around you were employees when you were young, you most likely grew up with the perception that in order to become successful, you needed a formal education. Get a good job in a solid company, work hard and be loyal, then retire with a good pension. Accordingly, with this background and these perceptions, you would be likely to reject at first an opportunity to start a business that "costs" $20,000, fearing the investment of capital and the time involved.

> *We are, to a large extent, a product of other people's habitual way of thinking.*

However, if you come from a home environment where your parents and others around you were entrepreneurs and ran their own businesses, you would be likely to see it from a different perspective. You would probably think that $20,000 is a very small investment with a short payback period and rich returns. You would be more likely to look for what's good with the opportunity rather than what's wrong, You would, for example, see that you could link to a brand name worth millions, have stock, marketing and other overhead costs taken care of by the provider of the opportunity and that this is "your chance," all depending on what perception you may have when starting your evaluation.

When you are in the position to make such decisions, ask yourself, "How can I see this from another perspective? What's good with this? How can I make it happen?" Rather than just look at it from one angle, see it from the opposite or other angles. Another natural law of the universe is The Law of Polarity, or the law of opposites. Whatever you look at, there is always an opposite side of the same thing; there wouldn't be anything bad with something if there weren't something good with it also, so why not look for the positive, and you will find it. If you only look for the negative in situations and people, you will find that too. Constantly look for the good in situations and people.

If you are a business executive or a business owner and reading this, you may want to consider these laws and make use of them in your thinking. You may also want to effectively teach this thought process within your organization. I am certain that The Law of Polarity and the Law of Relativity, when applied the right way, would strengthen a company's performance just as it strengthens the performance for any sports team or individual.

For the top athletes of today, where most techniques of physical and technical training are known to all competitors, effective use of this information may even be the "razor's edge" that make one individual or team rise above the others. Most people think that there must be huge change in activity in order to achieve improved results in life. My experience is that there often are small differences in activity, as small or thin as a "razor's edge," that make huge differences in results, whether we are referring to sports results, business results or results of a more personal nature. Bob Proctor illustrates this well and dedicates a full chapter to this subject in his best selling book *You Were Born Rich.*

It would be a mistake to underestimate the role of perception in our daily lives. It has the power to alter our attitude and course of direction almost without our notice. It takes much strength of will to change perceptions we have held for a long time.

Will

Will is our ability to concentrate and focus on any given task until it is fulfilled, regardless of outside forces trying to pull us away. This is where discipline comes into play. Some years ago when I started my first business and set a goal to become independent, I used my will to hold on to that image, despite all the forces around me that tried to talk me out of it. Most often when people come up against something they know very little about, they tend to first ridicule it, then reject it and even argue strongly against it. There were colleagues, headhunters, and friends who "warned" me. I thank my wonderful parents and sister who were always supportive and encouraged me that whatever I set my course to do, they would always support me.

Our will allows us to hold an image, idea, or thought that we want in our conscious mind until it has the chance to embed itself into our subconscious and manifest itself in our lives. It is much like a lens we can adjust and focus. How many of you, when you were young, used a magnifying glass to catch the sun's rays and focus that energy on a piece of paper until smoke appeared? Our will works in much the same way. It allows us to take any subconscious idea that may have been present in our minds since childhood and through intense concentration, change it. If we do this repeatedly over time, our subconscious is forever changed and altered for the better.

Imagination

This is our creative power. We have the ability to create airplanes, fax machines, the Internet, automobiles, and light bulbs against all doubt and odds because of the combined power of imagination with other intellectual skills. Your imagination is either imagining how you can do something or why you can't. You can consciously choose to focus on how you can and develop an "I can" attitude, which will make many areas of life go smoother.

It is with our imaginations that we dream and build pictures of how we want our lives to be. Setting goals is an intellectual exercise which can be learned. We use our imagination in the goal setting process to develop pictures of what we want. Make sure you use this intellectual muscle for your benefit, since it is very easy to do the opposite.

> *It is with our imaginations that we dream and build pictures of how we want our lives to be.*

I remember when I started playing golf and I was on my first eighteen-hole round. Coming to a par three hole, I placed the ball on the tee. Then I saw the "huge" body of water, which looked more like a lake between me and the green I aimed for. Par three means that I ideally would use not more than three strokes to get the ball in the hole. Seeing this "huge lake" and the very small green one hundred seventy meters away, I thought that I better not risk the new white ball, so I went back to the bag, picked up an old dirty ball that I had found somewhere, just in case I should hit the ball into the water. With that image in my mind, you can probably imagine what happened. I put another dirty old ball on the tee and tried again, and the same thing happened as before; the ball plopped into the center of the water. After the third ball disappeared beneath the lake, my friend, who has many years of golf experience, said with humor, "The water is not in play." Not understanding what he meant, I replied, "What do you mean 'not in play'? It is huge!" Then I understood what he meant. When I focused on the vastness of the water, that is directly where the ball landed, but when I built an image in my mind of the water not even existing, or being in play, and the ball sailing through the air to land on the green, that's what happened.

Unfortunately many people focus too much on building images and thinking of what they don't want to happen, hence attracting more of the same. Make sure you develop an "I can attitude," look for solutions rather than problems, and use your imagination to your benefit. Focus on building images in your mind of what you want to happen. We spend a lot of time thinking of what we don't want. What we think about, we get more of, or as Earl Nightingale put it so well:

"We become what we think about."

For example, none of us wants to be poor, have debt, or be stuck in a career we dislike; however, that is precisely what many people focus on. They say to themselves, "I need to get out of debt," instead of getting help to set up an automatic debt reduction program and focusing on the thought, "I want to increase my income."

Once you grasp the larger understanding of this concept, it becomes natural for you to shift your thought pattern. Mother Theresa was once asked if she would like to be part of an "anti-war campaign." She politely declined the offer by saying, "If you start a pro-peace campaign, I will join you." She understood that you get what you focus on. Make a decision to focus your thinking on what you want, rather than what you don't.

Allow yourself to think and dream of what you really want. Ask yourself if you dictate your life or if you let others dictate it for you, while excusing this fact by making statements like, "In life we must compromise."

> *Allow yourself to think and dream of what you really want.*

Memory

This is our ability to recall previous events and experiences. Many of us tend to remember only our failures, and those memories seem to linger much longer and be more intense than our memories of success. It is important to use our memory to bolster our confidence and self-esteem as we try something new because at some point everything was new to us, yet we learned.

> *We must exercise our memory to work in our favor and remind us that we can do anything we set our mind to.*

I used to play football (what Americans call "soccer") and was frequently the top scorer on our team. However, from time to time I had a period where I couldn't seem to put the ball into the goal, no matter how big the opportunity. After a couple of misses, I started thinking about the misses rather than the hundreds of goals I had scored earlier. As a result, I missed even more. That's when it is important to consciously use your memory to your benefit. I started focusing and thinking on all my past successes. I read old newspaper articles about the goals scored and the games won and before I knew it, I was back on track. Today, sports stars frequently use DVD/Video to watch their old successful plays and triumphs to speed the process along even faster.

We must exercise our memory to work in our favor and remind us that we can do anything we set our mind to. By consciously focusing on past success, no matter how small, it improves our overall self-confidence. Every person reading this book has succeeded at multiple things in life to get to this point. Whether you have won awards, received a promotion, or created lasting and loving relationships with those you love, claim those successes. Remember them every time you set your course for a new journey in life.

Chapter One
The Dream

Essential Tools

- **Imagine your life differently. If you can dream it, you can do it!**

- **Learn to *Think Wealthy*. You have the ability to control your thoughts.**

- **Practice the Mindset of Expansion.**

- **Understand the difference between knowing and doing.**

- **Learn to exercise your six Intellectual Faculties.**

Journal/Notes

Chapter Two

Life in Abundance

Stop

$25\frac{1}{2}$

Chapter Two

Life in Abundance

Out of Abundance, He took Abundance,

and still Abundance remained.

-The Upanishads

The word "abundance" literally means full to overflowing.
In reference to your life, abundance is much more than that; it is
never ending and always expanding. This can be a difficult concept
to process mentally because we are taught from a young age that
everything exists in a finite amount and can be depleted or "used
up." This is simply not so.

Imagine you are with a group of people and you all take a
deep breath and hold it. From the abundance of air, you all took
abundance, and yet air still remains in abundance. The mindset
of abundance is a realization that every person has access to a

fulfilling and wealthy life. It is not about some going without or "losing," while others are getting ahead and "winning." This is true in your work life, family life and your finances.

Think about the love a parent has at the birth of their first child. It is overwhelming and all-consuming. That love does not cease or become reduced at the birth of a second child. It expands. In fact, several parents have told me that it doubles and can continue to expand exponentially.

This abundance is also available in our work lives. If you have a great idea for your business, it does not decrease someone else's ability to have another great idea, it expands. The world we live in today is proof of the expansion and growth of idea upon idea. Would we be able to flip a switch and have light if not for the discovery of electricity, invention of the light bulb, and development of modern electrical generation and delivery systems? What about computers, cell phones, automobiles? All of these items have expanded abundantly from the first spark of an idea.

> *The world we live in today is proof of the expansion and growth of idea upon idea.*

In today's team-based work environment, most of you have probably experienced a work situation where a group of people come together to "brainstorm" ideas on how to accomplish a task. The synergy created by a group of people throwing out multiple ideas and rapidly exploring options will allow you to easily see that in fact, "two or more people can think more than you can on your own." In this case, you could easily see how one good idea could spark several other good ideas, and just because one person had a great idea, doesn't mean that we emptied the universe for good ideas. On the contrary, we became aware of even more great ideas, which is proof of the mindset of expansion.

I remember a time when I was in charge of international sales for a large travel corporation and we were about to lose one of our largest international clients. Our international network had not served the customer well for a while, and while they were happy with their Scandinavian solution, decisions were about to be taken in the client's world headquarters that were not in our favor. Many people in our company would lose their jobs and we would suffer severely if we had lost this client, so I was charged with the task of finding a way to save the account. We had ten weeks to present a new proposal.

I assembled a group of the best large account salespeople from our partners around the world in our Stockholm headquarters. For a couple of days, I lead the group through a brainstorming and discussion process. We came up with a plan that we immediately executed to impact the client's experience with our company on a worldwide basis. Two months later, after fifteen-hour workdays, seven days a week for some of us, we held a final presentation of our new offer to their top executives. A few days later, we received their response. Not only did we keep the business we had, but we were also asked to take on more countries, which enlarged our business with this client and provided jobs to many more people. This success can be attributed to a great team of people with a crystal clear goal, and it all started with one idea sparking off other great ideas until we had a plan and went to action.

In the normal process of doing business, most people think with a competitive mindset. This is a mindset of get what you can, be better than everyone else, and fight for the top position. However, as we can see with the idea of brainstorming, if more people would focus on being creative and think "expansion," more people and more businesses would win. Remember, in the universe there is abundance. The business world will not run out of clients, or money, or sales prospects just because one entity is successful. There is room for all to achieve success by thinking of how to expand business instead of maneuvering to keep each other out of the marketplace. I believe there is room for all to win.

The new way of thinking for today's corporate executive is to focus less on what everyone else is doing and more on getting his employees to work together. The old mindset of encouraging employees to compete among themselves is no longer effective or conducive to good results.

What about wealth? How can it possibly work in this same way? Money is just an object, a commodity. It has no power other than what we give it. Money has the ability to expand with abundance only to the extent our minds will allow it to expand.

For example, a person doesn't necessarily earn $50,000 a year because they want to earn $ 50,000 a year. More likely they earn $50,000 a year because they don't know how to earn $100,000 a year or more. Before you have made a decision to earn $1 million a year, you are not likely to think, create or attract ideas and solutions for how to earn $1 million. You will simply not think on that frequency. Why wouldn't a person decide to earn $1 million? If no one in the family had ever done it before and you grew up in an environment were no one ever did, you are not exposed to the idea of $1 million being within the realm of possibility and would probably not think in those terms. You have not been conditioned or programmed to think in abundance with respect to money.

> *Changing the paradigms of the subconscious mind is necessary in order to have any improvement to their results.*

Today we see many children grow up in an environment where parents and even grandparents and great-grandparents are or were living on social welfare. A German friend of mine told me a while ago that over one million children in Germany alone live in this environment today. They may very well grow up thinking that this is the normal way of living and this is how it's supposed to be. They will think lack and limitation are the norm and abundance and expansion are beyond them. Our big challenge is to increase their awareness that although they have been conditioned to think this way, they can change those paradigms if they choose to. Changing the paradigms of the subconscious mind is necessary in order to have any improvement to their results.

From people around you, you often hear expressions like these:

- Money doesn't make you happy.

- Money doesn't grow on trees.

- Do you think I am made of money?

That money doesn't make you happy is a ridiculous statement. Money was never meant to make you happy; remember, it only has the power that we choose to give it. Money is for two things: to make you comfortable and to provide better service to your fellow human beings far beyond what's possible with your physical presence. It is amazing how creative you can be if you don't need to worry about money. Money isn't an end unto itself; it is merely the means. Therefore, you should not work for money; you should work for satisfaction and provide service to earn money.

One of the laws of the universe is The Law of Compensation, which is always at work for all people in all situations. The Law of Compensation states that the money or compensation you will receive will be in direct proportion to the need for what you do, your ability to perform, and for the difficulty of replacing you.

> ## *You are either creating or disintegrating; you grow or you die.*

I remember some time ago on one of my business trips to Copenhagen, I woke up in the morning, turned on the TV news, and listened while getting ready. A man in his early sixties was being interviewed and he showed anger, frustration, and disappointment. His employer, a large brewery, had just announced that he and hundreds of his coworkers in a factory outside the city would lose their jobs as management had made the decision to move production elsewhere. He could not understand this decision due to the fact that the company had one of its best financial years in a long time. What he was not aware of was that management constantly has to look for ways to expand and improve the company's efforts to increase sales while holding cost as low as possible. That is how they represent the share owners' interests, who created his job in the first place, and those shareholders want a certain return on their investments. They are aware that you can never stand still. You are either creating or disintegrating; you grow or you die.

This is as true for people as it is for a business. In this case, the Law of Compensation had worked. There was a need for what this man was doing. He was probably good at what he was doing after having worked in this factory over thirty years, but it was so simple to replace him by shifting production to some other, more cost effective area that the company had no choice but to do so. You may ask yourself from time to time, "Is there a market for what I do, as a person? How about my company, the one I own or where I currently work? Is there a future market? How are my skills?" Whatever you do or decide to do today, become good at it! If you become really good, the difficulty of replacing you is much greater.

George Bernard Shaw once made a provocative statement when he said:

"It is a sin to be poor."

He also said:

"It is your duty to become rich."

He obviously meant that money is something you receive for service rendered. If you don't earn much, you cannot provide much useful service; hence his statement was correct. The problem does not lie with money; it lies within our own minds. Once you shift your mindset to one of abundance, every area of your life will experience expansion. The question is not, "How do I make more money?" but, "How do I change my mindset to one of abundance?" In order to understand how to change your thinking, you must first understand how the mind works.

Learning to Think

The mind is a powerful tool, yet few people ever consciously consider what creates our thought patterns, feelings and actions, and what is therefore responsible for the results they experience. The answer is attitude.

When we think of attitude, most people think of positive thinking or having a bright and cheery attitude. Whereas that is an important part of attitude, it is only a part of the truth. Attitude is a composite of your thoughts, feelings and actions, not one of the three, but all of them working together in combination. These thoughts, feelings, and actions are a product of our conditioned behavior, which includes how we were raised, the kind of education we were given, and people who have influenced our lives. We are all a product of our individual experiences; thus, each of us has a unique attitude. In order to understand how these ideas and actions have become ingrained into our behavior, we must understand how exactly we learn.

Everything we know, we have learned in four specific stages:

- Conscious Incompetence
- Unconscious Incompetence
- Conscious Competence
- Unconscious Competence.

To present this progression of learning, let's take the example of how a baby learns to walk and the stages of learning associated with that activity.

A baby first crawls in order to move around in his environment (unconscious incompetence). He soon develops the desire to walk and does so by holding firm to furniture and practicing (conscious incompetence). As the baby's walking improves, he is able to concentrate and take a few short steps (conscious competence). Soon the child is running, not even thinking about each step (unconscious competence). Once a process is learned, the mind moves it into the subconscious and it becomes a part of us that we no longer think about. This same process is at work when we learn to ride a bicycle, drive a car, or use a computer.

As human beings, we think in pictures. If I told you to think of your car, your home, or your family, instantly pictures of these things flash upon the screen of your mind. If I ask you to think of your mind, you have no picture. You might get a picture of your brain, but your brain is not your mind anymore than your fingernail is. Your mind exists in every cell of your body. It's hard to understand your mind and how it works unless we have a picture, so to illustrate and explain this process, we will be using the stick person example below developed in the 1930s by Dr Thurman Fleet in San Antonio Texas and made popular by Bob Proctor.

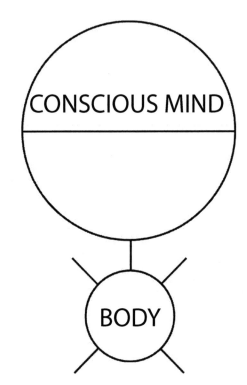

Conscious Mind

      The top circle represents the mind or thoughts, and the bottom circle represents your body or action. The mind is divided into the conscious and the subconscious. The conscious mind is where you receive all the input and experiences from your world. As you are faced with new events and ideas, your conscious mind has the ability to *accept* or *reject* any idea you choose. When thoughts come to you from your environment, the conscious mind is the filter that allows you to choose only those ideas and events you want to be emotionally involved with. The conscious mind is also where you create the dreams and goals that you want for your life.

It is estimated that today you and I are bombarded through multiple forms of media and experience with tens of thousands of images per day. Of these images we can effectively capture or process 1,000 on a conscious level. The information age has magnified the complexity of our lives while simultaneously making our lives more efficient and easy through technology. You are constantly choosing what your mind will process and be exposed to but, like most people, you probably don't realize it is a choice. If we are constantly inundated with negative messages, we will choose negative thoughts and ideas which will be stored in our subconscious mind. We then become a negative person with negative ideas and opinions. If we want to think, feel, and act more positively, we must guard our subconscious with our conscious mind by being watchful of what ideas we get emotionally involved with and what images we are repeatedly viewing.

> *The subconscious mind has no ability to accept or reject thoughts.*

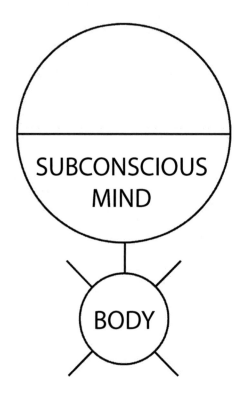

Subconscious Mind

This is the "emotional mind" or "feeling mind." The ancient Greeks called it "the heart of hearts." The subconscious mind only has one answer to all commands it receives from the conscious mind, and that answer is "YES!" In the smash-hit movie *The Secret,* James Arthur Ray tells us that it replies like a genie with, "Your wish is my command!"

The subconscious mind has no ability to accept or reject thoughts. This is why it is important to monitor thoughts and ideas as we receive them in our conscious mind. If we worry about something happening, then the subconscious will move us in the direction of having that negative thing happen.

Likewise, if we create a positive idea of how we want events to go or how we want to handle the unfortunate things that happen in our lives, then the subconscious mind can and will manifest that positive result.

I remember studying philosophy in the evenings after finishing high school while working full time and waiting to enter the military service. On the day of the exam as we walked in to get our assignments and get started, a student friend of mine said, "I hope they don't give us Descartes, and…." He went on and on about what he didn't want. Of course he attracted it and failed the exam, along with fifty percent of the others. The failure rate on this exam was known to be quite high, so that was also one of the things he focused on during his study time.

> *You will always attract more of the same energy that you are in harmony with.*

While I studied for this same exam, I had a full-time job at the local post office, played soccer five days a week, and did my best to maintain and develop a relationship with my girlfriend at the time. I had little time left over for studies, but I have been fortunate to have great parents and people around me that always encouraged me to think of how things could happen rather than becoming afraid of what might be. On this particular exam, there were around twenty philosophers they would choose from. I picked the seven most likely philosophers we would get this year based upon what they had presented in the last few years. There was a certain rhythm to the process. I learned these seven really well, knowing that we would get three choices from which we had to explain and discuss one of them. Going into the examination room, I felt calm, confident and ready. I expected to get one of these seven and didn't waste any time or energy on what might happen if none of the seven appeared. Two of the three choices listed where among the seven I had studied, and I received a top grade. Having an expectant attitude was the key. Worrying and focusing on what you don't want takes just as much energy and time, if not more, than focusing on what you do want. You will always attract more of the same energy that you are in harmony with. If the energy is negative, then that's what you will receive.

> *You must start mentally being the person you want to become.*

The encouraging message from understanding how the subconscious mind works is that we can monitor our conscious mind and, more importantly, use auto-suggestion to increase our positive results, as Napoleon Hill describes in *Think and Grow Rich.* Hill encourages us to create the thoughts and ideas that we want and, through repetition of those thoughts, they will become real in our lives.

Maxwell Maltz, M.D., penned the health and success classic *Psycho-Cybernetics* in 1960 and said:

"A human being always acts, feels, and performs in accordance with what he imagines to be true about himself and his environment. This is a basic and fundamental law of the mind. It is the way we were built."

It's been said that you can never outperform your self-image. What do you think of yourself? Why not imagine yourself wealthy, healthy and happy?

One example of this is that I have had people frequently tell me that they just can not seem to find a life partner. One friend said, "I don't seem to meet anyone." I can relate to that. Although I never had a problem meeting women, I couldn't seem to meet "the right one." It never bothered me much since I happen to really like my own company and enjoy spending time by myself with myself. Although I wondered some times why my relationships seldom lasted more than a short period of time, two to three years at the most, I felt good.

In retrospect, I must admit that in search for the optimal relationship, I had the tendency to see what was missing rather than what was right with the person. If there were one-hundred things about a woman that meant something, I could let myself be irritated by the five things that I didn't like rather than focusing on the ninety-five percent that was right. If you look for something bad with a situation or a person, you are guaranteed to find it. The Law of Polarity, or the Law of Opposites, states that there will always be an opposite in every situation. There wouldn't be an outside if there wasn't an inside to a room. There wouldn't be a top if there wasn't a bottom.

In Norway we have a saying that "there's nothing bad that doesn't bring something good with it." Why not start looking for the good things in people, situations and opportunities. At the same time, take an honest look at what you think of yourself. I really love myself and so should you, being the wonderful, unique person you are.

Some good questions to ask yourself that will give you an idea of what your self-image is right now are:

- Would you marry a person like yourself?

- Would you like to be working for, or with, a person like you?

- Would you strike up a conversation with someone who has your attitude?

- Would you like to come home to a spouse like you?

- Would you like to have a parent like you?

- Would you like to have a friend like you?

If you have a self-image of being a bad-looking, boring, terrible person, would you want to have anything to do with you? You must start mentally being the person you want to become, because you will only do or have the things you want if you first start being that person. Many people have it backward. These people often say, "If I only had an understanding wife, then I would do the things required and I would be a good husband." What they should think is, "I am a good husband; therefore, I do what's required in a relationship. As a result, we have a good marriage."

You see the same in many work places. Salespeople, for example, excuse poor results with, "If I only had a better district, better client base, and more leads, then I would do the action required, and I would be a great sales professional." But as Bill Gove so many times said, "A pro is at his best regardless." What the salesperson should say to himself is, "I am a professional salesperson; therefore, I do the action required and I have the sales results I want."

My sister Nina used to be a waitress many years ago, and I often visited her in the restaurant where she worked. It always puzzled me why she almost always had the biggest sales and the biggest commission. No matter what day of the week, which tables in the restaurant they served on, she always seemed to come out on top among all the servers working in the restaurant. Today I know the reason. She saw herself as a professional salesperson; she expected people to want more, so she always asked those extra questions and made the extra effort. She asked if they wanted a starter, sold them on the menu items and convinced them that dessert was not to be missed, followed by after-dinner coffee. She was a proud server and she knew it. Her clients felt her attitude as well and trusted her recommendations. Through studies, proper coaching and practice over years, she had grown into a great professional. She thought highly of herself and so did her clients.

A seminar I recommend highly if you or someone you know has a challenge with their self-image is Bob Proctor's program "The Winner's Image." This seminar will help you understand yourself better, and give you the tools to make the necessary adjustments in how you perceive yourself and how you are perceived by others.

When you and I get emotionally involved with a dream or goal and it enters the subconscious, the mind "locks in." Failure becomes negative feedback guidance to make a conscious correction and get back on course. This is comforting because the minute that you have your goal on the subconscious level, you cannot miss your target if you stay in action and don't change your setting.

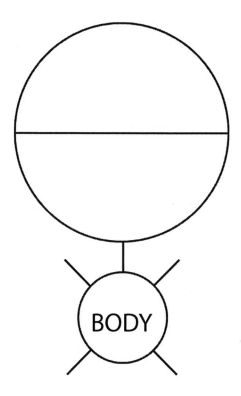

The Body

The body is the physical form and machine that is created and recreated daily by our dominant thoughts and actions. The body carries out actions based on directions from the conscious and subconscious mind. It is the evidence of what is held in the mind. For example, let's say you decide that you want to be a public speaker. If you worry about being nervous, saying something inappropriate, or are concerned that someone will make fun of you, then the body will manifest those thoughts. Your palms will sweat; you will stumble over words and feel very embarrassed. However, if you spend time imagining how positively your audience will respond, how articulate you will sound and how energized you will feel, the body will manifest that as well. You will be confident and full of energy, and your audience won't help but respond positively to you. When we change the thoughts we give the most focus and energy to, and repeat these thoughts until they become ideas, we alter the ideas that are impressed upon our subconscious mind, which again changes how we feel, act and respond.

Decision Making

Most people look at their current and past results and let that, together with information from the outside world received through our physical senses, steer their thinking and their decision making. We are never taught the art of decision making in school. When it comes to making a decision, we are conditioned to ask the people around us, "What do you think?" The fact is that most don't consciously think. We have opinions based on emotion, guess work, and often fear, but we don't actively and consciously consider a situation before we offer an opinion on it or make a decision about the best course of action. As Dr Ken Mc Farland once said, "Two percent think, three percent think they think, and ninety-five percent would rather die than think."

The reason so few of us actively think is that it is much easier to let our subconscious take over. To actively consider an event or course of action, you must push away the other thousands of images that are bombarding your conscious mind and focus.

Henry Ford put it best when he said, "Thinking is hard work; that's why so few engage in it." He's right. It is very hard work to change your habitual responses and emotions, and force yourself to consider alternative possibilities before making a decision.

Instead, we listen to what people say, or what we see in the news on TV or the Internet. Everyone has an opinion, and as Napoleon Hill points out in *Think and Grow Rich*, "Opinions are the cheapest commodities on earth." Nonetheless, it is amazing how strong people's opinions can be on subjects in which they have virtually no knowledge or experience. Even more surprising is how often we take advice from people about subjects that we should know that they know very little about, and still we let their advice decide our thinking and action.

This not only limits you to your own experience, but to the equally limited experience and opinions of others. For example, you may look at your bank account and let that dictate your opportunities for financial growth. When an opportunity comes along that excites you, and you ask others what they think about it, they will often respond negatively based on what they have heard or the opinions they have gathered, not on the facts. This is true in all areas of life. How often have you met those that let their past relationships dictate their belief in new relationships? When a new relationship comes along, how often do these same people ask others for advice only to be reminded of their own past failures? This is not active thinking and decision making.

Most people are not aware of how to think. We are taught *what* to think, but not *how* to think. If people are aware at all that we have intellectual faculties with which we can think and create whatever we want, they are often not using them properly. The faculties of Reasoning, Intuition, Perception, Will, Imagination, and Memory can be exercised. We can train ourselves to take control of our thinking and how we feel and act, thus controlling the results we get. Most people are actually using the intellectual faculties, these mental muscles, to their disadvantage. For example, memories of failure that are revisited repeatedly in the mind can convince even the most capable person that they are doomed to fail.

> *We are taught what to think, but not how to think.*

We see this in many areas. A salesperson misses a few sales and starts losing belief in himself instead of playing up the old memories when he did well in order to get back into that "vibration" of success. A relationship starts going bad, and the two people focus on the problems instead of remembering all the good things to again find the feeling which brought them together. A business person goes bankrupt and, instead of getting up and starting again, loses himself to the fresher memories of failure and deserts entrepreneurship completely instead of learning from the temporary setbacks and viewing them as just that - temporary.

If you know people in similar situations or who have similar experiences, do them a favor and encourage them to move on while remembering what they did well. If a person holds their first sales presentation and it's less than impressive, as the first time it seldom is, then focus on the positive. Encourage them to try again, while you give them the necessary suggestions for improvement.

The Comparison Paradox

I have come to the conclusion that money, like everything else, just "is." It only makes you more of what you already are; it doesn't change you. If you are a good person, it will make you a great person; if you are a bad person, more money will probably make you a terrible person. There are many examples of good people with a great deal of money giving much back to society, Bill Gates and Warren Buffet to mention a couple. Therefore, as a friend of mine once said, "If you consider yourself a good person, get rich!" Bob Proctor also states that, "The best thing you could do for poor people is to not become one of them." In other words, if you want to help others, help yourself first. You can not give what you do not have. So what is holding you back? Like many people, you probably suffer from what I call the comparison paradox.

It is natural for all of us to compare ourselves to those around us. Most of us carry around the idea that we are "average," meaning we are within a lifestyle that is comfortable and comparable to our friends, neighbors, parents and siblings. What it really means is that we are limiting ourselves through comparison to others. We create within our own minds an idea of what is "obtainable" rather than "possible." Thus, when we try to set goals, we start out by deciding what is obtainable and then take steps to achieve that limited goal. A good example would be if you look at your bank account and income statements of what you earned last year, which is what you know you can earn, then decide to stretch a little to what you think you can earn and set your goal there. This goal may only be five to twenty percent higher than last year. The problem isn't that you can't meet that goal; you can. It is that the goal is too limited to begin with, and instead of contemplating what you really want, you force yourself into a series of very small steps to reach what you think you can achieve.

This same idea is also at work in our relationships. You may be in a roomful of people, some very attractive and others more average. If you consider yourself average, you will only approach those you feel within your ability to attract and therefore may pass up a wonderful person who is your soul mate.

Not only is the comparison paradox active in our personal lives, it is frequently seen in the business arena as well. When I worked as an Executive Vice President in a large corporation, each year we would budget for the next year's sales. Normally we argued for a ten-percent increase. We knew the board and owners would ask for thirty percent and we usually ended up with a "goal" of twenty percent. This turned out to be a prognosis rather than a goal. Instead of striving to be number one in the market, we strove to improve upon last year's performance and limited ourselves in advance to no more than a twenty-percent increase at best. What if we'd aimed for the top even if it meant doubling our sales? The truth is we'll never know because we limited our possible achievements prior to even trying.

The problem with the comparison paradox is that when we compare ourselves to what we have always accomplished in the past and set goals from there, we believe that we are making progress, a good thing in most people's minds. In reality, it limits us to a predetermined outcome and cheats us of our true potential.

> *The truth is that ninety-seven percent of us don't even set goals at all.*

Chapter Two
Life in Abundance
Essential Tools

- Abundance is available to everyone in every area of life.

- The conscious mind has the ability to accept or reject any idea you choose.

- We can monitor our conscious thoughts to increase positive results.

- Your self-image determines your attitude.

- You must overcome conditioned thought in decision making.

- Beware the danger of the Comparison Paradox.

Journal/Notes

Chapter Three

The Point of Origin

23

Chapter Three

The Point of Origin

Nothing will ever be attempted if all possible objections must first be overcome.

- Samuel Johnson

Are you ready to envision a life that is possible rather than probable? Are you ready to improve your life echo in amazing ways? This will set you on a path of fulfillment and joy in every aspect of life, but only if you don't allow yourself to get caught up in the "how." Just imagine the life that you would want to lead. This may seem like a simplistic idea, but visualizing what you want helps solidify it in your mind. By imagining that you can live a wonderful life or create that perfect business, you place the image in your subconscious and it assists you in achieving that life or business.

There is an old saying that "The most difficult part of any journey is the first step." This is true, and you must take this step in faith to understand the "how." This is counterintuitive for most people. They have the idea that you should set a goal, make a very detailed plan on how every step will be accomplished, and then work toward that goal. However, this method requires that you dream of the best life possible, set out on the journey, and then watch for opportunities to make that vision happen. In order to have a different life, you must think about doing things differently and this includes escaping the habit of self-limiting goals.

The truth is that ninety-seven percent of us don't even set goals at all. We merely drift through life wishing that something good will happen to us, or at least hoping something bad won't. Goal setting is an example where everyone has an opinion, but few have actual experience. If only three percent of us are setting goals at all, then how can everyone have an opinion on how it should be done?

> *You make the decision, and then you will attract what you need to get your idea off the ground.*

By starting on the journey before you have all of the "hows" figured out, you avoid the comparison paradox and avoid limiting yourself to any preconceived ideas about how your goals should be accomplished. A strange phenomenon occurs when you make a decision. You attract opportunities to yourself and you also reveal who you are as a person. That decision resonates out from you and echoes back in the form of the tools and teachers you need to accomplish the goals.

I have met many people who have hesitated in the evaluation and decision phase of whether they should invest even small amounts in a business opportunity to chase their dream. People evaluate these kinds of situations very differently, and much of their core personalities come to the surface. If a person is not used to investing in a business, they will most often see the investment as a cost and hesitate, making excuses such as they don't have the money, can not afford it, etc. My experience is that until a decision is made, this person will never find the money, but when they make a decision and set out upon the path, all kinds of creative opportunities occur to allow them to finance the deal.

> *Opportunities seem to present themselves out of nowhere.*

I have several friends who have started their own businesses. The investments ranged from a few dollars to hundreds of thousands, even millions of dollars. The fact is that very few had the money when they made the decision. They made the decision and then they found the money. For example, a friend of mine wanting to invest five thousand dollars in a network marketing business asked ten friends to lend him five hundred dollars each. Within three months they all had their money back with interest, and my friend was off to a great start with a business taking off after a three-month return on investment (ROI)! Another person I know very well recently invested $250,000 in a business start up. When he made the decision, he attracted a business partner who had the money available. They started a fifty-fifth partnership, and his partner leant him the money for his share. Within six months they will have the ROI, and he will have paid the loaned amount back.

I once overheard a person asking my friend Bob Proctor, "I want to follow my dream and start this business, but where on earth shall I get the money?" Bob's answer was, "From wherever it is right now." He was right. You make the decision, and then you will attract what you need to get your idea off the ground. This is true, whether it is money or a business partner, the right job opportunity, the right mentor, or advice you need to fulfill what you want. You will start attracting what is in harmony with the energy you are in. After all, if you are hesitant to make a decision to go after a certain job position, why would anyone want to hire you? If you are uncertain whether you believe enough in a business opportunity to want to invest money in it, why would anyone else believe in it enough to lend you the money?

I remember twenty years ago when I was a student working for the IBM Corporation in New York on a year-long exchange program, I made the decision that I wanted to work for IBM upon my return to Norway since I thought this would be the best possible start in a profession within sales and marketing. I had no idea how it would happen, and I still had a year left to study when I returned to Norway. One evening I visited a bar and enjoyed a "happy hour" after work socializing with colleagues from around the world. I struck up a conversation with a gentleman standing at the bar while ordering some drinks. I invited him to join our table as he expressed that it looked like we had a great deal of fun. He turned out to be an IBM executive who worked in Paris and knew the top managers in IBM Norway. We got to know each other over the ensuing months, and he was very helpful in recommending me to a job with IBM in Norway.

> *I have met many people who have hesitated in the evaluation.*

Opportunities seem to present themselves out of nowhere. Why? Because those opportunities exist right now, but you are unable to see them if you have not set in your subconscious mind the idea of what you want. Therefore, you drift through life passing right by multiple opportunities yet never even being aware of them.

The concept of identifying goals and completing them depends upon the fact that you believe it is possible. So what is stopping most people? People develop their beliefs about what they can or can't accomplish from even the smallest incidents. A person I know quite well wanted to start a small home-based business and invest around $3000. Full of enthusiasm, she went home to her husband about this new idea that seemed to be exactly what she had been looking for and dreamt about. Her husband, however, was of another opinion. "Where are you going to get the money from? You have never been successful in business before, and you have no sales experience." He even found an article written in a newspaper about another person who once had tried something similar with another company and other products and had failed. He demanded, "What makes you think that you can do any better?" That was it for her. She retired back to safety, letting her husband "steal" her dream. To my knowledge, she is still unhappy with her situation and if anything, this episode just damaged their marriage.

You may have family or friends who constantly tell you to quit dreaming and be more realistic. But, you have to decide if you will allow others to put limits on your life. Who tells us which dreams are too big or how much money is too much? Knowing that you are in complete and total control of your own destiny, no matter what happens or what others say, gives you the freedom to find your true self and determine who you will become.

Honesty First

Our challenge is to not let past experiences and results steer our thinking and decision- making about the future. Any of you who have investments may have seen this disclaimer in very fine print: "Past performance is not a guarantee of future returns." Not only is this true in investing, it is true in our lives as well. Current and past experiences are only results of how you have been thinking and have nothing to do with the future.

It comes down to honesty. What are the brutal facts? Where are you today in all areas of life? Make a personal inventory, or a "checkup from neck up," as some would put it. You should view this as a starting point from which you will go forth into your future, not as a limitation to what you can accomplish. There is no point in regretting what's happened in the past; just learn from the experience and move on.

Many people fear and worry about things they can't impact or change. Earl Nightingale and Bob Proctor's *Lead the Field* states, "Research shows that people waste a great deal of time worrying about needless things.

92% of all the things we worry about are needless worries:

40% will never happen.

30% have already happened, and can't be changed.

12% are unfounded worries about our health.

10% are petty, miscellaneous worries.

Only 8% are real.

The key is to separate the real from the unnecessary and solve those which are within your ability to solve."

When I was a young boy, I feared going to the dentist based upon a less than pleasant experience I had when I was five years old. I would worry for six weeks before my appointment, only to find out that I had perfect teeth and nothing to worry about. A former colleague of mine spent much time in fear of losing his job as the company he was working for was downsizing. He almost got an ulcer in the process and his worries affected his family life. Soon his wife and children took on these worries too, only to find out a couple of months later that his division was not going to be affected at all.

Stepping into the Flow of Abundance

If a person wants to get out of the habit of worry and into the flow of abundance, how would he or she begin? A helpful exercise is to write down those things you wish to change in your life, even though you may feel it is not in your control to change them right now. Then you must strive to change the constant stream of negative thought running through your mind. Some of these may sound familiar:

- I am frustrated and unhappy with my work.

- I no longer want to spend time away from my children and family.

- I am tired of feeling financially strapped and want to improve my quality of life.

- I no longer want to feel less than adequate because I am not as successful as I think I should be.

Once you use this technique you will discover immediately how powerful positive thought is. You will also find that you are not really a victim in most circumstances except in your own mind. You have the power to change if you want to.

Besides these thoughts, we may also conquer negative behaviors or habits that limit our ability to believe in ourselves. For example, you may find that you have become an "excuse-maker." I once met a sixty-three year old person who was about to retire and worried himself sick about the small amount of money he would receive when he retired. I suggested he could start his own little business from home. I even had a concrete opportunity for him and suggested I could help him getting started. However, he excused himself by saying "I'm too old to start a new business now, and I am not a salesperson." I know a woman who started a similar business when she was sixty-five, also with no former business or sales experience. Today she is a millionaire at age seventy-five and enjoys herself more than ever running her own business from home and traveling the world while inspiring others.

Many times your excuses may sound something like these:

- I'm too tired to make big changes.

- I don't have enough time to figure out how to do this.

- I have too many other responsibilities.

- I'm too old.

- I'm too busy.

- I'm too young.

- I'm not a salesperson or business person.

- I have no money to invest.

Making excuses, like any other bad habit, can be hard to stop. This is why Alcoholics Anonymous has this saying, "There are a million excuses for picking up a drink, but no good reason." Are you excusing yourself from a great life? From making more money? From having the freedom to live as you choose? Excuses abound, but real reasons are few.

As you begin to use this self-monitoring technique, you will discover how powerful thought can be, whether it is positive or negative. You will feel more powerful to choose and adapt to changes that are right for you.

Self Image

Have you ever gone to the amusement park's funhouse and looked in the mirrors? If you have, then you are aware of how distorted and ridiculous the images can be. You look fat or thin, and there are mirrors that make your face seem long or short. Yet daily many people picture themselves with similar images. They may think, "I'm a loser," "I don't deserve this," or "I'm stupid."

> *Why do we believe the worst about ourselves and then perceive it to be our reality?*

Why does this happen? Why do we believe the worst about ourselves and then perceive it to be our reality? Why is it so hard to believe the best? The human mind is incredibly powerful and has amazing abilities to allow us to cope under all types of conditions, even in the most intense and adverse circumstances. If you constantly allow your internal critic to tell you that you aren't good enough or smart enough, eventually you will buy into that idea and believe it to be the truth, and your life will even begin to echo that fact back to you in every area! By viewing the world through negative filters, it is possible for you to fulfill your own negative predictions.

A friend I spent some time with when I was younger was not very good looking, but he was confident and had the self-esteem and self-image of himself as a "rock star." He always attracted pretty girls. At the same time, I knew another guy who looked very good, but was always negative to himself about his abilities and never missed an opportunity to express it to people around him. In addition, he blamed circumstances for his results and as the reason why he didn't achieve what he wanted in different areas. Naturally he attracted more negative results. The girls did their best to stay away from him so that they wouldn't be affected by his negative energy. When I heard years later that he was having problems at work and in his relationships, it didn't come as a big surprise.

In order to attract you have to be attractive, not necessarily physically, but emotionally. You have to have a positive outlook for anyone to want to spend time with you. This is also true in business. As a leader in your business, you must know where you are going with the business and be able to express it so that people will be attracted to join you. One of the absolutely most important tasks you have in any business is to attract and recruit the right people.

> *In order to attract you have be attractive, not necessarily physically, but emotionally.*

Between Christmas and New Year's a couple of years ago, I had a wonderful learning experience that illustrated this idea perfectly. I was on my way to Oslo, Norway, from a city in the middle of Sweden. Due to the heavy snowfall I was traveling by train, but even the trains had problems that day. I had to make a detour that included a couple of stops on my way. As I was waiting for the next train in a small city, the snow was coming down horizontally due to the strong wind, and the temperature was well below freezing. Suddenly an older lady came rushing past me through the snow while dragging her big suitcase in one hand and her walking stick in the other. She couldn't see much through her foggy glasses, and when I offered my help, she didn't seem to hear me.

The person driving the train was sitting with his window open, enjoying a cigarette, and the lady, while breathing heavily, stopped and asked him, "Excuse me, is this train going to Gothenburg?" The person looked at her and said with a calm and relaxed voice, "Yes, we are madam, and you have plenty of time. We leave in ten minutes." Now the lady seemed to register me, and excused herself while asking if I had talked to her. I repeated my offer to help her with her luggage and she accepted thankfully. She found her seat and suddenly looked very calm, knowing that she was on the right way. Now rewind a minute or two, and picture the situation again as she struggled through the snow, desperately wanting to reach the right train and asked the driver again if he was going to Gothenburg. What if he had said, "Well, I don't know, maybe, maybe not; maybe we should go to Copenhagen today, or up north?" Do you think the lady would have taken the chance and jumped on his train? Probably not; more likely she would have hesitated, then gone back to check before making any decision.

Now think about the business idea you have that you want to attract people to invest in, or the business you are running that you want to attract and recruit the right people to. Do you know where you are going? Are you able to express it in a crystal clear way so that you are attractive to those who might consider joining you?

The problem with allowing our perceptions to go unchecked or untested is that they can become our reality. There is an old saying, "A lie unchallenged soon becomes the truth," and our minds will make it so. It is also sometimes stated as, "If you tell a lie often enough, you will soon believe it." The problem is that the lies we tell are to ourselves. Have you allowed the perception of yourself to become so negative that you have stopped dreaming? Have you become so entangled in the struggle of everyday life - bills, kids, marriage, and work - that you do not see the opportunities that surround us all?

Breaking the cycle means to stop beating yourself up for past mistakes. Forgive yourself! You can learn from those harsh lessons and plan to do better in the future. If you have tried investing before and were left with nothing in your bank account, stop dwelling on it. Move on! Maybe you failed with a diet or exercise plan, and threw your hands up in the air with disgust at your lack of determination. Look at this as an opportunity to walk away from those past frustrations.

Now that you have decided to let go of the past and rid yourself of negative self-talk and excuses, you are ready to move forward. You are ready to learn a process about life and people, and to use your new skills for improving your life and increasing your net worth. You are also free to develop new, positive beliefs about yourself and visualize how your new life can be different.

You may be thinking, "That sounds great, but what will prevent the old negative thoughts and behaviors from creeping up again when things become difficult?" This is a valid concern. Many people experience a setback by allowing the "what-ifs" to run through their minds. These may include:

- What if I had tried harder in that relationship?

- What if I had not taken my spouse (or parents, children, friends) for granted?

- What if I had let someone else drive?

- What if I had told my kids I loved them more?

- What if I had not made a stupid mistake?

- What if I had finished school?

This type of destructive inner dialogue only gets worse with time, and can lead to paralyzing fear and indecision. If you don't let go of the past, it will keep growing until it overwhelms your present and destroys your future. Remember, that which you project will echo back to you. If those thoughts are destructive, that is what you will receive!

Indecision can be another destroying behavior. When working in the IT industry, I experienced a customer who hesitated to make a decision to buy, afraid of what would happen if they bought now and new technology came on the market next year. Then when next year came, he said the same. He wouldn't say no outright; he just postponed the decision. Suddenly, the company found themselves being passed by competition whose decision makers had advanced and won market share from them. The customers later expressed the fact that they left their old supplier because that company didn't seem to stay ahead of the game, and that their new supplier was able to deliver better solutions at a lower price and with better service. The person I had dealt with who was not able to make the decisions soon found himself without a job. After all, a company doesn't need decision makers who are unable to make decisions.

Like this man, many people are afraid of making the wrong decision, so they make no decisions and watch their life or business spin out of control. Focus on the solutions. Take out a piece of paper and write down every possible option you can think of. By allowing yourself to explore all the possibilities, you are moving forward.

You will be able to find better and faster solutions by performing this exercise than if you just worry. The key to dealing with the everyday stress of life is to force yourself forward. An important aspect in this process is our ability to set and achieve goals.

Goal setting and goal achieving are two different things. Goal setting is an intellectual exercise, a skill that can be learned. Goal achieving is a lawful process, and happens if you learn to use the natural laws of the universe to your advantage. One of these laws, the Law of Attraction, is particularly helpful.

> ## The Law of Attraction doesn't discriminate; it just delivers.

Law of Attraction

In the simplest terms, Law of Attraction says that what you focus your thoughts on every day, you will attract into your life. This is expressed as an overall law of the universe and does not recognize whether those things are positive or negative. This is why negative people tend to attract more negativity into their lives, and positive people attract more positive opportunities. When you think about this in terms of your life echo, you can easily see that just as negative or destructive thoughts return negativity to your life, positive thoughts bring abundance, joy, and fulfillment.

The Law of Attraction is an extension of the idea that everything is energy. The Law states that what you consistently think about and have emotions about will happen in your life. The emotions could be positive or negative. The Law of Attraction doesn't discriminate; it just delivers. If you want to bring something or someone into your life and focus your energy on that item or person, you will most likely get it. On the other hand, if you do not want something at all, and constantly worry and fear it might happen, it probably will. The Law simply states that whatever is most prominent in your awareness is most likely the actual thing you will attract. The way that this happens is through *focused thought* and through *feeling*.

> *Setting goals is an important part of the process of attracting what you want into your life.*

Thought is a form of energy, just like anything else. If you focus on that thought long enough, the object becomes "physical" and a reality in your life. We can liken this idea to an architect. The architect comes up with the idea for a new building. He focuses on the thought and sets pencil to paper, creating a drawing. That drawing is then presented to the client who approves the idea, and then the builders create the actual building. The process is the same for anything you bring into your life: from idea to focused thought and then to realization.

Setting goals is an important part of the process of attracting what you want into your life. You imagine your goal and your life as you would like to live it. You then set about finding others to help you and mentors who can teach you how to achieve your goals. You take action, all the while expecting the reality to materialize.

Your feelings will tell you what you are attracting. If you think and feel good, you will attract good things into your life. If you think and feel badly, you will attract negative things into your life. It's as simple as that. I used to be focused and give a little too much energy to what was wrong in a relationship rather than on the good, and for many years I remained a bachelor. As I stated in an earlier chapter, it didn't bother me, but the fact that it happened is still interesting. To me, my remaining alone was not good or bad, it "just was." What's interesting is that soon after I made a decision to be focused only on the positive with the person I am in a relationship with, I met Angelika, who later became my wife.

When I drive my car into the city on a busy day, I say to myself, "I wonder which parking space will open up for me today." Nine out of ten times, I get parking in the area I want. If it doesn't happen, I make sure to stop and think of why I was surprised this time. Last time it happened, I found what has become our favorite Argentinean restaurant in our hometown. Before I left the house that day, I remember saying to my wife that I could really stand to eat a good steak that day. Have you ever experienced thinking of another person and the fact that it's been a while since you last spoke, or that you would really like to talk with that person, and then that person calls you seconds after? When you are in harmony with the right energy, you will attract people, opportunities and the right circumstances for your ideas to manifest in physical form.

You can apply these principles in every area of your life. The following are the steps to follow that will allow you to harness the power of the universe and make your dream of success a reality.

Basic Principles

The Law of Attraction is actually a sub-law to the Law of Vibration. I like how Earl Nightingale and Bob Proctor in *New Lead in the Field* explain this law:

"The Law of Vibration decrees that nothing rests; everything is in a constant state of movement. Your physical body is a mass of molecules in a high state of vibration. It is moving so fast, it appears to be still. The truth is it is casting off and recreating millions of cells per second. Your body moves so fast it glows. Every cell of your body has a positive and a negative pole. The image in your mind will dictate the vibration that you are in at any given time and, of course, as the image changes, the vibration changes. Negative image – negative vibration. Positive image – positive vibration. Holding an image in your conscious mind has no effect on your life. However, when the image you are holding is turned over to your subconscious mind, your whole world begins to change."

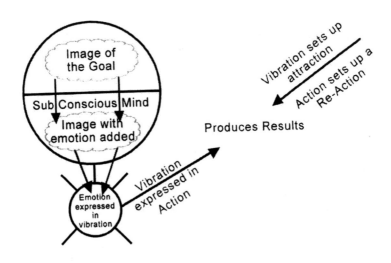

"*The conscious mind impresses the image upon the subconscious. Whatever's impressed must be expressed. The subconscious mind expresses itself through its polar opposite – the physical body in emotion. This emotion alters the vibration of the mind/body (vibration on a conscious level is referred to as feeling). The vibration expresses itself in action; your body literally moves into action. Every action sets up a re-action. Then, when you take into consideration that there is an attractive force at work in the universe, the only thing that you can attract to you is energy that vibrates in harmony with you. If you are in a negative vibration, you definitely will not attract positive people or situations into your life. They will, in fact, be repelled. However, if you are in a positive vibration, then everything of a like nature moves in your direction. This is the magnificent orderly process that is referred to as life.*"

This also explains "The Secret" that Ronda Byrne referred to in her bestselling DVD and book of same name. "The Secret" is The Law of Attraction, which is a sub-law that builds on The Law of Vibration. The vibration that we send out dictates what and who we will attract into our lives.

The Law of Attraction operates under these three simple principles:

- You ask. Just imagine a desire that you want for your life. What is it you want to be, do, and have? How are you going to feel once you have it? While this takes a little practice, don't limit yourself and dream big! If you want to start investing in real estate, for example, and earn $100,000 from it next year, ask for it! Set the goal!

- It is given. You receive. The Law of Attraction is universal; it delivers. Trust that everything you need will come to you as you set about seeking those who can help you.

- Allow and expect the result to come to you. This is where some people can get confused. This is about being prepared and being in harmony with what you want to receive. Our feelings play a major role in how much we allow ourselves to believe and how much faith we have in the laws of the universe. If we start off enthusiastically but then lose faith because we don't get the result soon enough, we're not allowing. If we want something but believe we don't deserve it, we are not allowing. If we desire something because we feel our lives will be a mess without it, we are not allowing since negative emotions will not attract a positive result. Focus on the end result, not the bumps and problems along the way. You will attract solutions to the problems as long as you focus on the end result.

If you feel good about what you want, you are drawing it to your experience. If, on the other hand, you feel bad about still not having what you want and frustrated that you aren't getting results faster, you are pushing your desire away.

Allowing is the state where you have the feeling of faith and expectancy about what you want. You trust that you will get it and you don't worry. You are not attached to the outcome. The state of allowing can be learned. It just takes a bit of effort and consistency, after which it will become part of your overall make-up.

When you consciously master the Law of Attraction, your life will be quite different – and much better. Not only will you create more of the things you want, you will also be better equipped to deal with situations you do not like.

Chapter Three
The Point of Origin

Essential Tools

- **Overcome the idea of how you have set goals in the past and dream big.**

- **Don't get sidetracked by the "how"; just make the decision.**

- **We spend too much time on needless worries.**

- **How to step into the flow of abundance.**

- **The Law of Attraction and how it works in your life.**

Journal/Notes

Chapter Four

The Destination

18

Chapter Four

The Destination

*"Never measure the height of a mountain
until you have reached the top.
Then you will see how low it was."*
                                    -Dag Hammarskjöld

What is your purpose? By that I mean, what were you meant to accomplish with your life? Just like ninety-seven percent of people don't set goals, an equally high number never even consider that they might have a purpose in life. A purpose, by definition, is a result or effect that is intended or desired. The words "intended or desired" are the ones that most people stumble over. In order to have a purpose for your life, you must think about and decide what that purpose is, and then desire its achievement. Having a purpose is to answer the "why" of your life.

As I stated in the introduction, my purpose is to inspire and encourage people all over the world that it is within their control to create their own future. It is my hope to inspire people to live their dreams while enjoying time and monetary freedom. I would challenge you to think about what your purpose might be. Evaluate your talents and desires. Realize that your purpose is to do the thing that you love.

> *You can make money from virtually any activity these days if you only open yourself to that idea.*

Some may scoff at this idea and say they will never earn a living doing what they love. This is an incorrect assumption. They assume, though most have never tried, that if you love a particular endeavor that it is inconsistent with earning money. They are wrong. You can make money from virtually any activity these days if you only open yourself to that idea. This is another example of allowing an assumption, comments from other people, or your own previous bad experiences get in the way of the truth. Allow yourself to focus on what you want without all the noise of "what-if." Let your mind dream freely of what your ultimate life purpose might be. It may be a good idea to set a side a day or two. Equip yourself with lots of paper and a couple of good pens.

When Angelika and I discovered our purpose, it didn't come as a result of an hour-long talk over a cup of coffee; it evolved over time. From the day we decided to formulate our purpose and put it on paper, there was a process of several weeks of thinking about it, discussing it and using half-day and one-day sessions writing and rewriting it before we landed on the wording that felt right, and this was just the "final touch." You don't have to rush this process, although I suggest you dedicate time to it and concentrate your efforts. Yet don't force it if you get stuck. In this case, it is better to rest a little while working on your wants and then go back to it when it feels right.

Angelika and I worked separately on our purpose and then discussed it together. We finally ended up with a purpose and a vision that we share. We also have common goals as well as individual goals. I would expect most couples to have separate purposes, as we are all individuals. It just happens that Angelika and I are very much alike and have chosen to work with similar concepts and businesses. We arrived at our purpose when we became aware of the fact that so many people live limited, unfulfilled lives. This is totally unnecessary, and only due to the fact that they think circumstances, conditions and their environment decide what they can be, do or have. Most have no awareness that their destiny lies completely in their hands. These people need to become aware of that power, and Angelika and I see it as a part of our purpose to spread this awareness.

Once you have a clear picture of your purpose, write it down. Consciously focus on fulfilling this purpose until it becomes a part of your subconscious mind. It is at that point you will develop a vision. Vision is the strategy behind the fulfillment of your purpose. It is the bridge between your daily goals and your lifelong purpose. Having a vision gives you direction and reveals opportunities that you have not previously been aware of. Once you have a vision and have started on the journey, then you can set short-term goals. You can also evaluate your life and cease activities that are not in line with your purpose.

Around fifteen years ago I came to a point where I decided it was not in harmony with my purpose to clean the house or to go shopping. It was a small part of my life, but I had always dreaded it. Since I hated doing these activities, I did them badly. So I made a conscious decision to not do them and paid someone else to do these tasks.

> *Once you have a vision and have started on the journey, then you can set short-term goals.*

When I met my wife, I explained that I did know how to do housework; I had done it for years prior to my decision. But in a relationship, there is an expectation of sharing the household duties. The way I saw it, we had two choices. One, we could continue to hire help. We pay a person who loves to have this job, does it well and enjoys getting paid to do it. They would do a much better job than me, in a fraction of the time it would take me to do it, and they would enjoy the work! On the other hand, Angelika could do it. There were certain things my wife enjoyed doing around the house and wanted to continue. This may not sound good to people who think that a man and his wife should share this work equally, but I can assure you that this solution works very well for us and that's important. We now use both solutions in that my wife chooses what she wants to do and what is in line with her purpose and goals; the rest of the duties we hire out. This way I free up time to do what I love doing and spend that time earning a lot more money than what I pay for the help we hire. We even get extra time off to relax and recharge.

What is it you love doing? Are you doing it, or are you spending a lot of time doing what you don't like, for a payment way below what you think you are worth? Do you have a purpose? Do you live in harmony with your purpose?

> ## *Do you have a purpose?*
> ## *Do you live in harmony with your purpose?*

We use this same principle in the area of business. My business is Life Success Nordic. We are a coaching, consulting and training company that takes the best products, skills and techniques to help individuals raise their levels of awareness in order to achieve better results in their personal and professional lives. Our stated purpose is that through personal coaching and public seminars, and by working closely with corporate clients, essentially serving as an extension of an in-house training staff, LifeSuccess Nordic brings its focus and expertise to help clients improve their results.

We frequently get new opportunities and by having a purpose for the company, it is easy to evaluate whether or not these opportunities align with our purpose, which determines whether we should pursue them or not. If they align, we'll consider the opportunity; if not, we won't.

> *I talk a great deal in this book about "balance."*

This is not to say everything is perfect. Sometimes we need to go out of balance for a period of time to achieve the balance we want. For example, you may work hard on starting up a new business. You put in much more work at the beginning to achieve a better and more balanced life down the road.

I talk a great deal in this book about "balance." However, this concept means different things to different people. You may perceive working forty hours a week as too much, whereas others don't even give it a thought because work is integrated into their lifestyle. They are on purpose and love what they are doing.

I know that some people think I work too much. I don't feel that I do, though this is just my perception. I do what I love doing; I am "on purpose" and work is integrated into my lifestyle. I seldom work more than thirty to forty hours a week, often less, and I have three to four months of vacation each year, although in some of these weeks, I may still chose to make phone calls and read emails.

As I write these words, it is morning in Spain. I got up around 7:30, had a fresh cup of coffee while I read the morning news and had some time to think. I set aside time at least five days a week to think. After that, I was out for an hour to look at a couple of investment opportunities before sitting to write this chapter. Around midday, I will stay by the pool and catch some sun, read a little, make a couple of phone calls and spend time with my wife. In the evening we will go to one of our favorite restaurants in the area for dinner before winding down at home. This is a working day when I am in Spain. If I sum up the actual work time, it could be around three to five hours. To me this is a lifestyle, working when I feel like it and having private time when I feel like it. To others who just see glimpses of my life, the perception might be, "Poor man, he has to work when he is on vacation." In truth, I am here for a month this time, and I can only take so much sun.

Another example of balance is when I worked in the IT industry within sales/marketing and management consulting. I often had sixty-hour work weeks, but I enjoyed that also for a time.

I still enjoy working and consider myself far from lazy. It happens from time to time that I go on the road and travel for a period of ten days at a stretch. Though I do work during that time, I also have a lot fun. I might have five full-day seminars and a number of other sales presentations on this trip in four different languages in several countries, while meeting a number of interesting people. The days may be filled from morning to evening with meetings, yet I don't feel tired because I love what I am doing.

You must decide your own definition of a balanced life. Do not listen to those who would tell you what you should do or how you should do it. I do know that if you want a different balance and a different lifestyle than what you are experiencing today, you must make a decision right now to change. A friend of mine once shared this quote with me, "The definition of insanity is to continue doing the same things and expect different results." If you want your life or your business to enjoy different results down the road, you must prepare for them. I came to the conclusion that if I wanted my life to look differently five years down the road, I had to make the decision right then and there to change my life and then look for ways to make it happen.

The problem is most people get so hung up on "how" that they never take that first step. "How" doesn't matter in the moment you make the decision. You will never know exactly how until you have taken the first step; only then will it happen. I have never seen anyone find out how they will earn a million dollars per year until they have made a decision to make a million. You decide where you want to travel on vacation, and then you find the best way to get there. Before the decision is made, you will not start searching and attracting the right solutions.

> *Your comfort zone is the lifestyle that you have become accustomed to.*

The Comfort Zone

As human beings, it is in our nature to risk. The challenge is that we have been conditioned by our environment to play it safe. While the internal part of us needs to test ourselves and grow, our belief system and current paradigms attempt to offset this desire to take chances, which results in inaction. The more conditioned we are by people and things around us, the bigger challenge we face to break away.

Your comfort zone is the lifestyle that you have become accustomed to. It is where you feel safe and "comfortable." Anyone who has studied physics knows that it takes much more energy to get an object moving than it does to keep it moving. Once we fall into our personal comfort zone, we cease moving.

We get used to our surroundings and actively choose not to leave. We reason that it's better play to it safe rather than step out into the great unknown. We worry about what other people will think if we risk and fail.

When I considered getting involved in a network marketing business a number of years ago, I had no experience in the industry. After having looked at it, I thought it made a lot of sense. The more I studied the industry and the more understanding I gained, the more I liked it. What a way to run a business! With a small investment you can buy into a brand name, have products you use and show with no major overhead costs. For example, the network marketing company would pay for research and development; they would finance the stock, distribution of products, and a number of administrative or organizational matters like marketing material, magazines, IT and management information system. As a distributor, you are the sales and marketing arm of the company, and your compensation is as fair as it can be, as it is in direct relation to your results. When you add the unbelievable opportunity for personal development, the learning experience is phenomenal, especially in the area of sales and leadership, in which the opportunity is huge and the investment is so extremely low that anyone can take part in it.

After discovering this business, I mentioned rather enthusiastically my newfound marketing opportunity to a number of people. I remember in particular one person that would have been perfect for it. She liked it, she wanted it, and we agreed to get her started. I would help her get her business off the ground. When we were to meet a couple of days later, she didn't show up. I contacted her to clarify a possible misunderstanding in regard to the agreed meeting, and she gave me all sorts of excuses. When I calmed her down and asked for the truth, she told me the real reason she had changed her mind was that her husband and two friends talked her out of it. The most interesting thing about this situation was that these three people had no knowledge of or experience with the industry or the company. They "had heard," however, of a distant acquaintance who once was unlucky with a network marketing opportunity years ago.

Now, let me ask this: Do you remember the so called "dot. com" era toward the end of the 1990s? There were many internet startup companies, and some real scams with no real substance, but people threw money into them hoping to become rich and some did. What if you had done this and lost as many people did? Does that mean that there is something wrong with the whole IT industry? Does that mean that IBM and Hewlett Packard are bad companies also? Of course it doesn't. This person was talked out of a fantastic opportunity with a solid IBM caliber company in the network marketing industry and missed it because she was more concerned about what other people thought than what she really wanted. She allowed them to steal her dream, and she will probably continue to let people steal her other dreams until she comes up with something that's in harmony with what they think. The fact that she turned it down didn't severely change my life, but

I felt sorry for her as it didn't change hers, either, and it could have. There is a significant opportunity cost when you pass up a dream based on someone else's opinion.

The Law of Polarity states that there are always two sides to the same thing; there wouldn't be a top if there was no bottom. There wouldn't be an inside to your house if there were no outside, and there wouldn't be something good if there wasn't something bad with it. If you come across an opportunity that is in harmony with your purpose, look for what's positive and what's good with it, and you will find it.

> *There is a significant opportunity cost when you pass up a dream based on someone else's opinion.*

I once saw a statement the founder of The Body Shop expressed when being asked for the secret to her success. Her answer was, "I look at what all the others are doing in my industry, and then I do the exact opposite." Remember the phrase, "No one is willing to die your death, so why would you let them live your life?" Don't worry so much about what other people think. As a matter of fact, it is none of your business what other people think. As a matter of fact, most of the time they don't really think at all and, as in this case, they were just "going to old movies" by regurgitating the preconceived ideas and training they had received throughout their lives. Most people are just echoing in their lives where they currently are, and it has nothing to do with where you want to go.

> ## *"No one is willing to die your death, so why would you let them live your life?"*

Once we understand that risk is natural, and to risk intelligently is what we are supposed to do to have a fulfilling life, we can be more consciously aware of and ignore the external forces that will hinder us. It takes a shift in our thought process to create enough desire to move beyond the safety of what we have known.

Have you ever asked a group of people, "If you had your life to live all over again, what would you do different?" I have, and I received many answers such as, "I would have married my high school sweetheart," or "I would have spent more time with my children." Then I asked a more specific question, "When you were faced with a decision that involved risk, the kind that made you uncomfortable and took courage to act upon, what did you do?" Some replied they took on the challenge; others replied that they did not act and reverted to safety.

Of the ones that risked, they all expressed that they were glad. Some even said they wished they had risked more and risked earlier in their life. Of the ones that reverted back to their comfort zone, they unanimously said, if given a second chance, they would jump at the opportunity to take that risk. In many of these individuals, the regret was so great that I saw their whole body language and facial expression change. They realized in hindsight that the world of uncertainty they saw, the world that compelled them not to act, was actually not that uncertain after all. It only *appeared* uncertain due to their self-limiting beliefs and other peoples' beliefs that they accepted as their own. In hindsight, they saw that they would have in all probability accomplished much more, and would have led more fulfilled lives.

We are all in some way a product of other people's habitual way of thinking. Your closest relatives probably loved you and wanted to do their best, but could not give you what they did not have. So the "bad news" is that they programmed you to a large extent to be the person you are. The "good news" is that they might have produced you, but it's in your hands to change whatever you want to change. My environment mostly conditioned me to believe that success would to a large extent be in relation to a good education, working hard, and being loyal to a big company, for which I would receive a good pension. When I decided that I wanted to start my own business, I was lucky to have a father who also had started his own little business after years of being employed, and both he and my mother always supported whatever I decided to do. When I decided to start on my own, I felt a certain uneasiness. I went through some mixed emotions before I finally overcame the fear regarding the risk of finally breaking with the pattern of thought I had all my life. I wish I had done it earlier, but

I have made peace with it, enjoying the fruits of my energy and not letting the past bother me.

When you find a worthy ideal, there will undoubtedly be a certain feeling of "uneasiness" that you experience. If you are not used to taking risks, then your mind will respond to this foreign concept taking root in your subconscious. It is similar to a tug of war that takes place in the mind of fear versus risk. Fear may attempt to stop you, and if you allow it, it certainly will.

If you search for reasons why a particular endeavor is not wise, you will certainly find plenty of them. Conversely, if you search for and focus on the rewards, your mind will find plenty of benefits. You must focus on the rewards. The more you hold the images of the reward in your mind, the more you silence that inner cynic called fear.

You can have fear without risk, but you can't have risk without fear. With this understanding, know that fear is natural and even healthy as long as it does not paralyze.

Utilize fear as your ally. Use it in such a manner that it compels you to do your due diligence. However, also realize that the stars will never line up perfectly. If you are waiting for this, you will be saying, "If only I would have…" many years from now. After you've done your homework, you must trust your intuition and take decisive action.

When taking intelligent risks, you will find the results justify the risks taken. The challenge most people have is that they have an aversion to risk. However, this aversion is not natural; it is learned. We have been conditioned since birth to "take the safe route" and it's "better to be safe than sorry."

> *When taking intelligent risks, you will find the results justify the risks taken.*

Think back to when you were a young child, or observe babies today. Risk is embraced and a natural part of their being. When you were a child, you thought big. Your ideas were big. You thought you could do anything. Some of us even thought we were Superman, capable of anything. The word "impossible" did not exist in our vocabulary. As we got older, most of us were overwhelmed by outside influences, stifling this natural urge to risk. Now, most must struggle to overcome this conditioning in every area of their lives.

One of my favorite stories is about Richard Branson, founder of the Virgin Group. He is a self-made billionaire and founder of Virgin Records and Virgin Airways, as well as the CEO of a conglomerate of some three-hundred and fifty companies. He started a hugely successful record company, knowing nothing about records at the time. He then took his passion for risk and started an airline, again knowing nothing about the airline business. His approach to life is simple, but one worth noting: Without risk there is really no great reward. His philosophy on risk is one of a global nature, not just business. He has made it a habit to question conventional wisdom, as conventional wisdom is typically made up of others' paradigms which have threaded in them the aversion to risk. He understood that being uncommon in his approach to life was the way to riches and a fulfilled life.

Richard Branson was a high school dropout. He had no special business training. He had the basic intellectual faculties that we all possess. What he did was to use his faculties of imagination and intuition, and became aware of business opportunities. But that's only half of the equation; he also took action and was willing to step out of his comfort zone.

Richard Branson can be described as being in the top one-percent of the population. He's in that "uncommon" group. If you think of a pyramid, the one-percent group can be described as the risk takers and are at the top. There's plenty of room at the top of this pyramid, while it is very crowded at the bottom. However, consider this: Although the one-percent club is exclusive by percentage, membership is open to each and every one of us. It's open to all who are willing to do the things that most people are conditioned not to do. It's open to those who are willing to embrace new ideas of what is possible, and refuse to live a life that is probable.

If we truly seek rich rewards in all areas of our lives, we cannot follow the crowd. We must be uncommon in our philosophy and approach. The uncommon understand that nothing is impossible, if backed by a definite desire and on purpose with what they want for their life. Risk is not an issue. As our desire and passion increases, what may appear as "risk" to an outsider is really not risk at all. It is moving forward with confidence and decisive action as we visualize the rewards that await us.

> *If we truly seek rich rewards in all areas of our lives, we cannot follow the crowd.*

Choose a purpose for your life that you are passionate about and step out into the unknown. Follow your vision and as the path becomes clear, set your goals for achievement. Once on the journey, revel in your newfound balance and freedom!

Chapter Four
The Destination

Essential Tools

- **Find the true purpose for your life.**

- **Once you know your purpose, seek balance in your life.**

- **Break free of the comfort zone and dare to risk.**

- **We must learn that risk is a natural part of our existence.**

- **Do not let fear convince you to take the safe route.**

Journal/Notes

Chapter Five

The Teacher

Chapter Five

The Teacher

"If you could find out what the most successful people did in any area and then you did the same thing over and over, you'd eventually get the same result they do."

— *Brian Tracy*

As you take the first step toward your new life, there are people who can help you along the way. By visualizing the kind of person you want to be, you will become aware of individuals who are already living that dream. Just knowing these people and asking for their help can shorten your learning curve and accelerate your progress. The role of a mentor, life coach, or mastermind partner cannot be underestimated, as the synergy created by those who have a like mindset can push you farther than you imagine. As we have already talked about, you project your new mindset, and these coaches and mentors are attracted to that. They are the evidence that your life echo has improved.

However, understand that this is about working on "you," not about taking shortcuts. The only way to conquer your past paradigms and change your ingrained habits is through studying over a period of time, while being guided by a good coach. Repetition is the key to all learning. Just as you learned to get dressed, tie your shoes, ride a bike, and so forth, you must learn how to strive toward your purpose. By spending time with a mentor or coach, you will be able to practice the mindset you eventually want to achieve. They can open your awareness up to possibilities that you never dreamed existed, and encourage you to act and get the results you want. Through studies combined with proper coaching over a period of time, you will gain understanding, raise your level of awareness, change paradigms, alter behaviors and catapult your results.

> *By spending time with a mentor or coach, you will be able to practice the mindset you eventually want to achieve.*

Norway's only world-class golfer is Suzann Pettersen. She has enormous talent and has worked very hard. She has also struggled the last couple of years to break through on the PGA tour in America, and has had problems with injuries. Many players in her situation would probably have given up at some point. Seen from the outside, it is impressive what she has accomplished this year. According to media, she renewed most, if not her whole coaching team, from physical and technical trainers to mental coaches. She has built a team of people to support her, and this year she won the LPGA Championship, her first major, a great performance and a great moment in the history of Norwegian sports. She also won another tournament and has held many other top positions. As I am writing this, she is number seven on the money list for this year on the tour. Through studying her profession, exercising, and training diligently under great supervision, she has broken through to become one of the world's best female golf players.

> *I made a decision a long time ago not to waste my time on people who wanted to do things their way.*

You may think, "Great, bring on the coach!" However, in order to benefit from a coach or mentor, it is important to do what they say in exactly the way they intend and not try to improve upon or change their advice. This may seem obvious, but my experience is that many people would like to be coached "their way." I remember when Bob Proctor agreed to coach me. He had one condition: I had to do what he told me to do. It made sense to me. After all, I wanted his results; it was not his wanting mine.

I made a decision a long time ago not to waste my time on people who wanted to do things their way. I suggest you do the same. If you ask someone to coach you, be prepared to do what they tell you to do in the way they tell you to do it, as long as it is moral, ethical, and legal. Only until you have proven that it doesn't work for you can you try something else.

Unfortunately, some think of a coach as a "garbage box" where you empty your frustrations, and a scapegoat to be used as an excuse for failing results, such as, "My coach wasn't any good." A mentor or life coach can really help you if you listen to them with the right intent; that is, if you really want their help and are ready to listen and implement their strategies. If you think about it, any big accomplishment by any person or team usually had a great coach involved, whether we talk about sports, business or life in general.

Personal Accountability

You may think that you have tried to change in the past, but nothing worked. Why? One of the reasons may have been that you kept breaking the commitments you made to yourself and then finding excuses for why it's not your fault. If this sounds at all familiar, it may be because you see yourself as a victim of your circumstances and feel like you don't have a choice. In order to change your life you must understand that you do have a choice, and with this choice comes a strong sense of personal accountability.

Some people think that accountability has to do with placing blame, which is not true. Accountability really means doing what you say you're going to do. It's simple, but not easy. If it were, people wouldn't so often fail to keep their commitments. And that's unfortunate, because accountability can totally transform your life. It makes everything possible.

The main reason that people resist accountability is out of fear. First, we associate accountability with blame. If we're accountable for something, we'll be the one to get blamed if it goes wrong. Second, we fear failure. No one wants to look bad, make mistakes, or feel incompetent. To avoid feeling that way, we don't challenge ourselves. Finally, we avoid accountability for fear of success. If we increase accountability, we will accomplish more, we'll be held to a higher standard of performance, and we'll have to maintain excellence. It is much easier to dream of success than to actually achieve it.

A few years ago, one of my salespeople held herself back from taking the next step in her development. On several occasions, she was on the verge of being promoted then something happened. I found out by talking with her that she feared the success of achieving the next level in the organization because she would have to take on more responsibility, expectations would rise, and she wouldn't be able to live up to those new expectations. If you have had a problem with personal accountability in the past, there are several steps you can take to overcome it.

1. Reject the Victim Syndrome

There is a quote by Voltaire that says, "No snowflake in an avalanche ever feels responsible." When things happen to you and you don't feel you have a choice in the matter, it sets up a victim mentality. The unsettling truth is that people usually choose to be victims. It's a mindset. Simply stated, when faced with a situation, you ignore, deny, blame, rationalize, resist, and ultimately hide from the problem.

For example, people who smoke and drink too much will often rationalize their behavior by blaming the stress they suffer, their boss at work, being a lonely mother, and other such excuses. A friend of mine got fired from his managerial position in a fairly large company. For some time he blamed his employer, his colleagues, the economy and everything around him for the fact that he ended up in this unfortunate position without a job. He is still without a job, and his attitude would have to change in order to become attractive to another employer. Another friend of mine in a similar situation took responsibility and the attitude that "this could be the best that ever happened to me." He saw it as an opportunity to become independent. Today he owns three businesses and earns more money every month than he previously did per year.

> *Breaking free of the victim mindset allows you to move into action.*

When you move from being a victim to being accountable, you realize that regardless of what has happened to you in the past, you can choose what to do next. Breaking free of the victim mindset allows you to move into action. In this way you regain power over a life that seems to be passing you by.

2. Take Control of Your Life

Now that you've stopped being a victim, you must clarify what real success looks like to you. Define your purpose, vision, and goals. When Jim Carrey was a struggling actor in the mid-1980s, he wrote himself a check in the amount of $10 million "for acting services rendered." Once you have defined your purpose and refined your vision of success, put together a list of accountable goals that will take you there. Yet beware of one of the surprising pitfalls of accountability: perfectionism. That's right. If you wait until you have perfected something, you will never move on. Remember what John Updike said, "Perfectionism is the enemy of creation." Or as Wolfgang Sonnenburg, a friend and mentor of mine, said to me when I got a little too analytical and wanted to discuss all kinds of strategies for going into a new business, "Progress before perfection; start with what you have. In the beginning it can be better to think less and do more."

> *Don't judge yourself or others or let resentment or guilt take over*

3. Be Honest

Until you know what you are dealing with and are willing to be honest, you can't do anything differently. Sometimes, a problem can look very big. When you shine the light on it though, it turns out the problem wasn't as big as you feared. So take an objective and unbiased look at where you really are. The challenge is to attain a neutral frame of mind, marked by compassion, openness, and sincerity. Don't judge yourself or others or let resentment or guilt take over. Your best thinking brought you to this point. If you had known how to do any better, you would have done it. Your current reality is a starting point for learning.

4. Take Ownership

Consider this: when you own something, you are much more likely to respect it. When was the last time you took a rental car through the car wash? Never? When you are working on a project with other people, assume one-hundred percent of the ownership in your own mind. Don't become a power-hungry dictator who takes all the credit, or a martyr who takes all the blame, or a sidestepper who takes none of the blame. Find a good balance of responsibilities, while keeping in mind that at the end of the day, what needs to be done, needs to be done.

> *Leave your ego at the door*

5. Embrace Forgiveness

"The old law of 'an eye for an eye' leaves everybody blind." -Martin Luther King, Jr. Once you have recognized the reality of your circumstance and take ownership of the part you have played in getting there, forgiveness is your way out. It is not an excuse to do something that doesn't work, but an opportunity to wipe the slate clean and give it another try. Forgiveness is not a substitute for corrective action, but a way to come to the action in a more creative, caring way. If a thought serves you, it is welcome to stay. If it paralyzes you, it has to go. Period.

6. Self Evaluation

This is the turning point. From here, you can start creating your new life. It's time to get rid of your automatic pilot syndrome which is thinking, doing, and feeling the same things over and over, and instead, start making deliberate, healthful choices. You may feel that you have no control over your circumstances, and it's certainly true that you can't control other people. What you can control is how you respond and react. Ask yourself, "How might I have created, promoted, or allowed the situation I am in?" If you are honest, you will see that you did play a role in your current situation, even if you merely sat back and let it happen.

A couple of years ago I was inspired by an interesting story I heard about an American woman who suddenly became owner of the family business when her husband passed away. The story and the method that comes with it has helped me a great deal with the point of self evaluation and taking a "personal inventory" on how I treat my life and my business.

The woman's late husband had been running their family business for many years and she had never been involved. To all others around her, the woman was said to know little about the business, and upon his death people expected she would sell it. When she announced that she would visit with the management team, they assumed it was to announce the sale. On the contrary, she asked to meet all managers separately.

She asked each one of them the same three questions: first, what are you doing, second, what works, and third, what doesn't? Then she empowered them to stop doing what doesn't work and do more of what was working or find new solutions to what didn't work. She came back week after week and rehearsed these questions with the management team, and they started doing the same with their employees. This simple method created an inspired organization who catapulted their results. I use the same method in private situations as well as in running my business, and so can you. You could, for example, in a marriage or relationship ask yourself, "How do we ignite and renew the excitement in our relationship? What are we doing; what's working and what isn't?" You could equally implement the same process in a sales organization by asking yourselves how to increase the sales two-hundred percent over the next twelve months.

7. Never Cease to Learn

Seize the opportunity and let yourself be transformed. Think differently. If what you did in a previous situation didn't work out, the process of learning guarantees you will proceed differently next time. Leave your ego at the door. To be a master learner, you must believe that you know nothing. In this way, you are able to replace old paradigms and learn from your new coach or mentor. In order to learn, you need to have just enough self-esteem. Too little self-esteem and you don't think you can learn; too much and you think you don't need to learn.

One of my teachers in business school suggested that he should put a stamp on my forehead as I graduated saying, "Best before _____" and a date, indicating that I would soon be outdated if I stopped learning. He said, "If you think you are finished learning when you leave this school, you aren't finished learning. You are just finished, out of date and not attractive. Not as a person and not as an employee."

8. Take Action

To like your life, the sum of your actions, you have to like each action individually. Take small, manageable actions that take you beyond your comfort zone but don't paralyze you. Keep moving toward your goal. Reach out for help when you need it. If there's one certainty in life, it's that things will not go according to plan! Knowing this, you also understand why you shouldn't wait for all to be perfect before acting. Act with what you have and make corrections while underway.

> *Take small, manageable actions that take you beyond your comfort zone but don't paralyze you*

Let me give you and example of what I mean. I have a friend who has never started his own business. He has thought about it for a while. He produces Excel spreadsheets, he plans and strategizes in detail while waiting for the timing to be "just right," but he never does it. The truth is that you will probably never have the exact right timing or the perfect economy, so just start it!

To be wise, you should anticipate how things may not go as planned. So decide what you'll do when you get off course. As long as you recommit yourself to your purpose, you will be able to recover from your mistakes.

Ultimately, there is no end or limit to the rewards of a life lived with personal accountability. Anyone who longs for the freedom should heed that message. When you commit to accountability, everything else falls into place. Your relationships become deeper, more honest, and more fulfilling. Your career takes off. Your health improves. Accountability unleashes your creativity and expands your ability to love and be loved. The accountable person knows that anything is possible and is not afraid to get out there and achieve it.

Personal Responsibility

When we take responsibility for our lives, we admit that we are the ones responsible for the choices we make. We, not other people or events, are responsible for the way we think and feel. It is our life, and we are in charge of it. We are free to enjoy it or disdain it. While we are not responsible for all that happens to us, we are responsible for how we think, feel, and respond to all things, both good and bad.

Many people associate responsibility with duty and obligations, which, in turn, are thought of as burdens. But personal responsibility is not a burden; it is a gift. This becomes clear when we understand that personal responsibility is nothing but the freedom to create our own lives. Once we awaken to this fact, we are liberated and empowered. We shed the victim mentality and gain the power to transform ourselves.

As a young student around twenty years ago, I was fortunate to take part in an international student exchange program called AIESEC. The program lets companies all over the world search for students to come work for them over a period of six weeks to eighteen months, and students may apply for jobs in other countries to achieve international experience. Through an advanced computer program, a computer matches students with jobs, and I was matched to a one year job with a consulting firm in Augsburg, a city in South Germany that was about an hour outside Munich. A few weeks before I was supposed to go, a manager of this company called me and explained there had been a mistake. They needed a person who spoke fluent German.

My intention for going there was to learn German as well as the profession. I could now have blamed the student organization, the computer, the German economy, my teachers, and so forth, but fortunately I took personal responsibility for the situation. I made a list of companies and cities around the world where I wanted to work and decided on IBM in New York. I contacted the local student organization and asked for the possibilities. The woman replied, "This must be your lucky day. We just got an application that states they need an extra person in the marketing strategies division in White Plains, New York, just north of Manhattan." I faxed over an application matching what they were asking for and three weeks later, I was there. I had one of the most wonderful years of my life there, a year that formed much of who I am today personally as well as professionally. I went on to begin a career with IBM and a fantastic learning process after I graduated from business school. I can't think of a better place to start a sales and marketing profession. What I learned about sales, leadership and management consulting in my seven years with this company gave me the perfect preparation for being selected by a large travel corporation to join their executive team responsible for all international sales. All of this happened because I chose to take personal responsibility for the situation and attracted the job with IBM in New York.

Why reject the roles of creativity, flexibility, and resiliency in order to play the role of victim? Why choose to be weak when one can be strong? Why choose to be sullen when one can be thrilled?

Let's get personal and talk about you for a moment. Are you perfectly happy with the way things are at this time, or do you wish things were better? Chances are, you are neither perfectly happy nor completely unhappy, for most of us lie somewhere between both extremes.

> *Change your choices and actions, and you will change the results that follow.*

If you wish to change, why not begin by recognizing that your present situation is not the result of your genes, parents, education, job, luck, timing, health, or environment. Rather, it is the result of choices you have made and the actions you have taken that have brought you where you are today. Change your choices and actions, and you will change the results that follow.

Examine your life to learn the extent that you are either already taking responsibility or evading it.

Do you ever say to yourself any of the following?

- Life is so unfair.

- I'm unlucky.

- No one wants to help me.

- It's not my fault that I'm the way I am.

- Life is an endless struggle; there are too many burdens to bear.

- Terrible things are always happening to me.

- My parents (or spouse, friends, coworkers, boss, health, the weather, or the political situation) make me depressed (or angry or frustrated).

- I feel overwhelmed and helpless.

- Some people get all the breaks; I'm just unfortunate.

This list is endless. Instead of taking personal responsibility and taking charge of your life, people who engage into this kind of thinking blame others life for their own failures.

Of course, it's easy to shift the responsibility and blame others or events. But what good is that? All it does is keep us in our comfort zone, and allow us or those we know to continue to echo negatively. We cannot make any real progress until we admit to ourselves that, "Only I can hold myself back. Only I can stand in my own way. Only I can help myself. Only I can take personal responsibility. Only I can transform myself from a victim of circumstances to a reasoning, decision making, action-oriented person. Only I can take charge of my life."

One of the first people we greet each morning is our reflection in the mirror. Don't we want to be accountable, answerable, and responsible for the life we are creating for ourselves? By accepting that responsibility, we unleash great power and transform ourselves. Though it may be hard to accept the fact that no one limits your options but you, it is a necessary part of the process of change. The ability to grasp the power hidden inside is one that few people ever find.

> *Happiness is a choice, just like misery is; we all have the responsibility to make the right choices.*

This emphasis on making the right choices and accepting personal responsibility is for your benefit only. That is, you must use these ideas to improve yourself but not to judge others. You can never enter the mind, heart, and body of another, so you are unaware of the reasons for their failures. Not everyone is as ready to change as you are. Happiness is a choice, just like misery is; we all have the responsibility to make the right choices. We owe it to ourselves to do so. Though once you understand this principle, you may experience some frustration as you see coworkers, family members, and friends continue to exhibit this behavior.

In life we have many choices; one is to take one-hundred percent responsibility for whatever happens in your life, as well as in your business if you are leading one. There is no point in blaming circumstances, environment, or conditions. Playing the victim while blaming the economy of the country, your family background or the politicians and the society for your results won't get you anywhere.

I learned from my wife that it is my responsibility to make me happy. It is not my responsibility to make her happy; that's her responsibility. By having that attitude, we have, as an example, a very clear direct communication without either of us feeling "hurt." We state what we want in all situations, not what we think the other one would like to hear.

I suggest you make the same decision for yourself. It is your responsibility to have a fulfilling life and to be happy, not your wife's or husband's, or the government's, or your parents' responsibility. Your employees or the financial performance of your company are also not to blame. Being accountable and accepting responsibility for where you are in life allows you to be open to the teachings of a great mentor and move along the path to success at a rapid pace.

Chapter Five
The Teacher

Essential Tools

- **Find a mentor to help guide your path and listen!**

- **Accept personal accountability in all areas of your life.**

- **Reject the victim syndrome.**

- **Take ownership of your choices.**

- **Embrace forgiveness and move on.**

- **Take personal responsibility for your life and the changes you want to make.**

Journal/Notes

Chapter Six

The Journey

Chapter Six

The Journey

"Determination is the wake-up call
to the human will."

— Anthony (Tony) Robbins

The idea of an abundant life is very attractive. Many people would like to seek abundance, but feel stuck in their current position. You may know some individuals who truly need a big change, or you may know someone who is just a bit unsatisfied, as I was when I set upon the path of personal development.

In this chapter we will discuss the idea of multiple sources of income and how networking can help you achieve your goals. You don't have to change jobs or quit your job to create a better life. You can start creating that life right now.

Most people only have one source of income: their present job. For many, that job does not offer the money or time freedom to live the way they choose. I have a number of friends who feel "stuck" in the sense that they are currently trading their time for money. Most of them trade all their working hours with one employer, and there is a natural limit to their income since there are a finite number of hours in each day. With all the possibilities there are today and the high price levels in our part of the world, there are a number of things people in this situation are prohibited from doing, everything from eating in a good restaurant whenever they choose to traveling away for the weekend. Multiple Sources of Income (MSI) is a concept that will permit you to multiply your current income and earn many times what you are presently earning.

Multiple Sources of Income is exactly what it implies: income from multiple sources. An MSI is not another job or a better job. In fact, it has nothing to do with exchanging your time for money. It has to do with creating ideas that produce income without your direct or constant involvement. MSIs might include activities such as real estate investing, writing a book, network marketing, and web-based affiliate programs. The list of available opportunities is endless and open to any person with enough creativity and determination to find them.

An important point to consider when you create an MSI is that you want to focus on creating "passive" sources of income as often as possible. By passive, I mean that it shouldn't take a lot of your time or energy. You want to create situations where you receive money on a regular basis because you contributed in some way, but aren't actively involved on a daily basis. Granted, there may be an initial output of time and energy to get things started, and it may or may not be extensive, depending on the MSI. But after that startup phase, it should continue to earn money without your direct intervention.

Thoreau once said, "If a person advances confidently in the direction of their dream and endeavors to live the life they have imagined, they will meet with success unexpected in common hours." I believe the key word in that quote is "endeavors." In other words, your goals may not be met perfectly. All you have to do is give them your best effort. Imagine your life of abundance unfolding in front of you and keep yourself on task, with your ultimate purpose at the forefront. Build a picture in your mind of exactly how you want to live, and then attempt to live that way. Don't look at your dreams as something that are going to happen in the far and distant future; look at them as something that already exist.

> *Build a picture in your mind of exactly how you want to live, and then attempt to live that way.*

Most financial worries are caused when a person tries to make decisions before they have sufficient knowledge. Their mind is clouded with negatives and "what-ifs." For this reason it could be very easy for you to doubt. Doubting your ability to multiply your income is natural because you have existed in your current situation for so long. You must visualize the end result and know where you're going in order to get there.

Another idea that goes with creating an MSI is that you must give in order to receive. This probably sounds backward to you. We have been programmed our entire lives to go out and get. Get a degree, get a job, and get married. It seems we're completely focused on what we can accumulate. This is an attitude of scarcity, as if the world will run out of assets so we must get ours. In reality, if we invest and project the right positive attitude and energy, that same positive energy is going to come back to us, often several times over. Generosity of spirit is always rewarded. Letting go of an attitude of "get" is hard at first but, with a little practice, you will find it fulfilling.

When you think of doubling or tripling your income, the idea has much to overcome within your mind before you will believe it can be so. If the most you have ever earned in a year is $50,000 or $100,000, that's an indication of where your subconscious mind is programmed. What you earn is an expression of your subconscious, a conditioned way of thinking about yourself and your ability to earn money. I would encourage you to focus on changing that limiting mindset.

Many years ago I remember dating a nurse. She was, and probably still is, a very nice person with a service-minded attitude. One day while we spent some time together, she told me that she would have a meeting next day with her manager at the hospital. The purpose of the meeting was to discuss her salary for the coming year. She asked me what I thought she could ask for. Her current salary at the time was $2600 per month. She asked me if I thought she could ask for a three-percent increase. I wanted to challenge her to think a little bigger, so I asked, "Why don't you ask for $2800?"

She looked at me as if I was the dumbest man on earth and asked me if I could be serious. When I said I was, she got a little irritated and told me that it was totally unrealistic and that I didn't understand. I started asking her some questions, and it turns out she has the finest nursing education you can get in Sweden from the finest schools. She had ten years of wide experience in the best possible hospitals. Her employer was in desperate need for her because there was a lack of nurses, especially with her background. In addition she was good-looking and had a pleasant personality.

Asking for $2800 would probably have given her a much better financial situation. However, her conditioning from the environment she had lived in her whole life prevented her from asking. Her parents were workers with low-to-medium income jobs, and most of her friends were nurses and police or firemen. They were all in a similar income range with similar conditioning. She came back after the meeting next day and thanked me for the conversation which had made her dare to ask for a three percent raise, and gladly told me that she had gotten a two and a half percent raise.. I guess the most important part was that she felt proud and happy, and that her employer was happy too. I still think she was worth a lot more and that they would gladly have paid her what she was worth if she had given them the chance.

My wife Angelika had similar programming and a low salary background, but she had worked eight years as a secretary for a very generous owner and boss, our friend Wolfgang Sonnenburg. He let her develop herself through practice, courses and seminars, and always gave her challenges and possibilities to stretch outside her comfort zone. She also worked during these years in an environment where she was handling large sums of money and where people were business and sales-oriented, and not afraid of thinking big. This made it easier for her to think big, and when the opportunity came to start her own business, she was not afraid of large numbers. The image she built in her mind helped steer her toward a tremendously successful business.

To get your MSI idea up and running, you must push your behavior into overdrive by developing new habits and new ways of thinking. To induce ideas and assist with getting your mind flowing in the direction of abundance, I suggest that you do some research on the many affiliate programs that are available to anyone and everyone. The internet can be a powerful tool, and an affiliate program offers very few entry barriers. They are easy to start and require no specialized knowledge.

Another popular area for creating income is through real estate investing. Property ownership not only can create positive cash flow, it increases net worth. This is an MSI where you can benefit from a good mentor. Find someone who is an experienced real estate investor and ask them how you can get started in the business. Learn from their mistakes and do what they advise.

You might also investigate various network marketing opportunities. I have found this particular avenue to be an honest, respectable, and great way to build a business that has unlimited possibilities. Often when I mention network marketing, the idea is met with suspicion and negativity. Many people have developed the idea that network marketing is bad either through a friend's disappointing experience or their own. Just because you may read about some scam in the paper on occasion, or hear negative comments from those around you, doesn't mean a whole industry is bad.

> *Make up your mind to start thinking for yourself and not let information from outside sources steer your decision making.*

Make up your mind to start thinking for yourself and not let information from outside sources steer your decision making. If you let outside forces decide for you, you'd better be one-hundred percent sure that the people you are talking to have phenomenal results in all areas of life! Collect information through your senses, but be sure that those you seek advice from those who have the results to back it up.

As with any idea that has the potential to produce additional income, you get out of it what you put in. Many times a person's past failed attempts had nothing to do with the business opportunity; it was because that particular opportunity wasn't in line with their purpose, vision and goals.

Belief

The first person who must believe in an idea is you. You must have the attitude of success and believe passionately and wholeheartedly in what you are doing. Set your goals and have the strength to move toward them in an efficient and consistent manner.

Let's take the example of wanting to learn more about real estate investing. You make an appointment and get to know a broker who can teach you about the business and also introduce you to others. Perhaps he introduces you to several realtors and a couple of other investors who are doing exactly what you would like to do.

Make no mistake, these people will watch you very closely for any clue that you may not be serious or sincere. If they sense that you are looking for easy money or are not willing to put in the time to learn, then don't expect them to return your calls. How you present yourself to your new contacts and connections is vital if you want to reach your goals.

Once they have seen you in action and know that you are sincere, they will take your education in the business up a level. They will share secrets that they would never divulge to an insincere beginner. This will speed you ahead on your path and increase your income much faster than if you tried to figure out the business on your own. They may also become potential business partners and co-investors at some point, so you must never underestimate the power of their opinions.

By growing your circle of contacts, you become a connection point for an increasing number of like-minded people. During the spring of 2006, I heard my good friend and mentor Bob Proctor mention that he wanted to set up licensees around the world and attract more people to teach his ideas. I agreed it was a great idea because there is a great need for this knowledge. After a dialogue about this over a few months, I decided to start LifeSuccess Nordic and go into business with Bob, together with my good friend and business partner Henning Hverven.

The ideas that I've learned from Bob, and have experienced myself, are important to teach to as many people as possible. We are attracting people every week who are joining our Nordic teaching team because they have a similar purpose for their lives. In Norway, Sweden, Denmark, Finland and Iceland, people and companies will get access to a number of learning possibilities through open seminars and coaching as well as company-specific training.

When this opportunity came, the decision was easy to make since it was totally in harmony with my purpose.

You may be presented with numerous other opportunities for investment and gain, but you must be very careful about which ones you choose. You purpose, vision and goals should always be your guide.

> *Each time you interact with someone new, it is like opening the door to potentially thousands of new people.*

The Leverage of Networking

You have to think of the people you know as your own personal spider web. Some are closer, such as your friends and family, and others are more distant, such as coworkers and acquaintances. You must work continually to add more rings to your own personal web. Most people know an average of about two- hundred and fifty people. These are friends, relatives, coworkers, past and present neighbors, church friends, former school mates, and such. Now if you know two-hundred and fifty people, and they each know two-hundred and fifty people, and they each know two-hundred and fifty people, then you see the unlimited potential. You grow your ability to influence people exponentially with every new contact, friend and business acquaintance you meet. Each time you interact with someone new, it is like opening the door to potentially thousands of new people. This network increases your leverage in the business world and opens countless doors, which is why network marketing is so effective.

One misconception that many people have about their network of contacts is that those closest to you are the most beneficial. In fact, just the opposite is true. Those you have weak ties to can often produce more networking connections than those closest to you. The reason being that the people closest to you have many of the *same* contacts in common. They know very few people that don't already know you. However, your acquaintances and coworkers come from all walks of life and all different geographical areas. They will have a completely different set of people to influence and give you more leverage over time.

It is a learned skill to seek out and maintain ties with your weak contacts. You must put forth the effort to maintain the relationship. One way to do this is to offer something free that is of value to that network of people. For example, if you agree to speak at a conference for free or little pay, they are grateful but will also allow you access to their entire network of members or contacts. This network becomes a group of individuals that you can now call acquaintances. You can offer more to these acquaintances by suggesting they sign up for your email newsletter. This maintains the contact and rather than just forgetting about you in a week or two, they are receiving a good, useful newsletter from you each month.

Using the contacts you know and the new ones you make, you can start a multitude of businesses from a consulting business to a network marketing business. Many people who are very successful have a variety of businesses and investments that are built one on top of another. For example, let's say you start a consulting business and also book numerous speaking engagements to promote your business. You can gather information from attendees and offer them a newsletter on your website. Each month as they visit your website for the updated newsletter, they can also buy products from your network marketing business or through various affiliate programs which pay you for the amount of products sold. You can then use part of that money to diversify and invest in real estate or joint ventures with other business partners. This is how empires are built: one step at a time through multiple streams of income.

There are many different paths you can take to reach your goals, and these are but a few suggestions. Once you have taken the first step, opportunities will open to you that are in line with your purpose.

> *This is how empires are built: one step at a time through multiple streams of income.*

A friend of mine started a business a few years ago
and became fairly successful. Soon after, he encountered some
obstacles, lost focus and belief, and the business took a dive.
He eventually gave the business up. Recently he started another
business, and I asked him why he thought this one would be any
more successful than the last. He gave me a great answer: "In the
previous business, I was in love with the result of what that business
would provide. I wanted to earn a lot of money. Now I love what I
am doing, and the money follows." He is "on purpose" and in line
with his vision and goals. I have no doubt he will succeed this time
and not allow temporary setbacks to discourage him.

Having worked as a management consultant, I have seen
many companies in numerous industries and to this date, I have
never seen any industry or company grow continually in a direct
upward path. There are always challenges along the way.

One of the universal laws is the Law of Rhythm. It states
that just as the tides go in and out, every area of life or business
has both good times and bad. As I mentioned earlier, you should
understand that these times will happen and be prepared for them.

The Person You Wish to Be

As you set your mind toward your ultimate purpose, you
will also realize tremendous personal growth. Individuals who
open themselves to all that is possible soon discover that they wish
to acquire certain desirable traits. These include honesty, integrity
humility, and a grateful attitude. Striving to incorporate these

traits into all areas of your life leads to balance and a feeling of fulfillment. This permanently changes not only what you project each and every day, but also what echo you receive back.

One of the ways you can choose to acquire these traits is by becoming a "Person of Quality." This means defining the qualities that you wish to emulate and focusing on them, setting them into your subconscious mind. Understand that these traits do not just happen. They require forethought, planning and effort. The following is a list of specific traits that you may choose to incorporate into your life.

5 Traits of a Person of Quality

- Have a strong desire to succeed mixed with personal humility. There is no need to shout to the world about your accomplishments. Determine a path and pursue it; those around you will see the progress of your efforts and note them without you ever saying a word.

- Act with calm, quiet determination and adhere to high personal standards. A person of quality works with calm, quiet determination and honesty toward what they want.

- Frequently sit back to reflect on events, never blaming others or outside conditions for poor results. A person of quality evaluates both positive and negative outcomes, and ponders how to improve. There should be no room

for blaming circumstance or other individuals for
problems. You must meet problems head on and deal
with them in the most positive way possible. Remember
Bob Proctor's words to me when I once was "stuck"
and had some problems in developing my business the
way I wanted. He said, "When faced with problems,
the person you need to talk to is always available for
consultation – just take a look in the mirror." You may
want to seek help to get "unstuck," but you must first
assume responsibility for the situation and not blame
other people and circumstances for your results.

• Don't be afraid to give credit to others. It is wise to
give credit to those around you for their help on your
journey of success. As a result, more individuals who
are impressed by your work ethic will join in to help
as well. They know they will be recognized for their
efforts and have no fear they will be blamed for a bad
result. This gives them the freedom to give one-hundred
percent.

• Work with diligence and do not be swayed by the "next
big thing." Adhere to your purpose, vision and goals,
and work toward them with consistent diligence. Do
not be swayed by a new money-making scheme, diet or
potential "opportunity of a lifetime." I have seen many
people temporarily a little "stuck" in their business
choose the easy way out, giving up the current business

and jumping on the next great idea that comes along. They rarely ever succeed anywhere. They seem to almost make it, then jump on the next popular thing. I suggest you really make an effort to understand the Law of Rhythm and make it work in your favor. There is a natural rhythm in our lives and in everything we do, including a business. You have good times and bad times. When you know you are on a down swing, do not feel bad. Know the swing will change and things will get better. There are good times coming, so think of them. Focus on the good and put things in the right perspective. You will gradually gravitate towards improvement.

Becoming a person of quality sounds easy, but it is not. It requires careful thought, planning, and constant evaluation. In order to incorporate these traits into your life, you can use the following four-step process:

- Confront Reality

- Remove the Negative

- Focus on Your Plan

- Lead a Disciplined Lifestyle

Step 1: Confront Reality

As you try to implement these principles into your life, you will be confronted with your former reality in the guise of well-meaning friends and family. This includes those who are skeptical of change, those who can't understand your need for change, and even those who hasten to point out every misstep and setback that you have along the road. Unfortunately, many times the people engaging in this behavior are the ones closest to you. Those whom you expect to support you maybe the very ones who put obstacles in your path. Personally, I am very fortunate to have a wife, parents and sister who were all the time encouraging and inspiring me. I have, however, seen many people's dream get "stolen" by those nearest and dearest to them.

I tell you this only by way of warning. You must be prepared and think about how you will handle these situations in advance. This will allow you to adhere to your Person of Quality (POQ) principles and not overreact. If your spouse, parents or friends constantly point out flaws or make fun of your plan, you have to be able to respond to the criticism in a positive way and still move forward. One way to do this is to allow them to have their say, and then ask for their help. If you allow them to help you toward your dream, then they have a piece of ownership in that dream as well. While they may be your worst critics at first, as they see your success and hear you credit them for helping, they will oftentimes become your biggest supports and fans.

For each area of your life you must confront the reality that exists in order to deal with it. This includes your work, relationships and lifestyle. You can have a positive influence on the people around you, but you can not change them.

> *You can have a positive influence on the people around you, but you can not change them.*

Step 2: Remove the Negative

This is one of the toughest areas you will have to confront. The reason being that it usually involves people, including those you care deeply about. You can get away from a negative work environment by changing jobs. You can get away from negative friends and acquaintances by relocating to a different area or city. But you can't get away from family and those you love. The relationships you have had and want to keep are the ones that you will have to confront and work on. What people have little knowledge about, they will tend to ridicule, resist or argue against. Some good advice I got when starting a new business was that "your success will be in direct proportion to the kind of books you read, the CDs you listen to and the people you surround yourself with." As mentioned, I have been fortunate with support from nearest family. I have, however, during certain periods been a little selective with which friends to spend more or less time with. This principle is especially important during the startup phase of a company or the launch of an idea where you only need positive energy around you in the form of people who just encourage you and root for you.

Unfortunately, I have witnessed couples that split up and friendships be challenged and even break in similar situations. Usually, these relationships were weak from the beginning and this was the final drop. Most of these people that would challenge and even work against you in these situations fear that you will "leave" them. Some fear that you will mentally develop into a stronger person and that you will get new and more interesting friends.

What we need to understand in these situations is that if you suddenly aspire to leave the masses or break out from the environment you're currently in, it may be uncomfortable for you, but you can be sure that it is just as uncomfortable for the people around you. We see this frequently in work situations as well, such as when a good salesperson, who earlier was "one of the guys," suddenly is being promoted to sales manager and now has to lead the others. They treat him differently and react differently, almost as if he were a traitor rather than a friend.

We see it in families when a person with a so-called "normal" job suddenly becomes president of a company, and the rest of the broader family and friends fear that the promotion will make him or her "too good for us." They start to see you develop and if they feel they're not, they could become uncomfortable with the situation. This is particularly important to handle and communicate well if it is your life partner.

Therefore, you should sit down and evaluate the relationship with every family member or friend and decide if they are an overall positive or negative influence. Do certain members of your immediate family make you feel like you aren't good enough or that you will fail at everything you try? Do they constantly speak badly of others and rarely have anything good to say?

On the other hand, are there family members who are constantly supportive and uplifting? Do they offer ideas and suggestions? Do you find yourself at ease and able to laugh in their company?

Though you can't change other people, you will know who the positive influences in your life are. While I don't recommend abandoning your family, I would suggest that, at least on a temporary basis, you spend a little less time with those who are consistently negative and practice positive reactions to their negative comments and behaviors. Spend more time with those in your life who are positive and soak up the positive energy and emotions. Those will carry you through many setbacks as you put your plan into motion.

As you become more confident over time, you will be able to spend time around negative people without letting them affect you. You may also be able to slowly change some of their own attitudes and beliefs, but even if you don't, *you* will have changed and that is what is important.

3: Focus on Your Plan

No matter what your goals or objectives, there will be setback and missteps. It is very easy to give up on your plan after one of these missteps and go back to life as you have previously known it. Change is hard, and there will be times you will want to take the easiest path. Remember the Law of Rhythm and that good times are coming. The Law of Polarity will also help you in this situation by knowing that if something is bad with anything or anyone, there also has to be something good. Look for the good in people and situations, and focus on finding solutions. You must decide right now that you will stick to your purpose. Instead of dwelling on the failure or negative event, imagine yourself taking charge and overcoming. The best way to focus on any plan is by action. By actively moving toward a goal, you feel in control and are allowing yourself to find the solutions.

> *Look for the good in people and situations, and focus on finding solutions.*

4: Disciplined Lifestyle

I think everyone views the word "discipline" with apprehension. Most think it is synonymous with hard work, which it is. But discipline not only involves the work you do, it also pertains to the life you lead. Many times, what you do is not near as important as what you don't do.

> ## *The first aspect of a new, disciplined you is the ability to say no.*

We already talked about that fact that one of the biggest complaints people have today is stress, but most of their stress is self-inflicted. They make bad choices, overload their schedules, and do what is the easiest instead of what is best.

The first aspect of a new, disciplined you is the ability to say no. It is okay to say no to your friends, your family, your spouse, your children, to anyone. Not saying no just tells others that your time isn't worth anything. You are always available no matter what hardship is placed on your family or your long-term goals. You have to stop the cycle of worthlessness by saying no.

Indeed, your time is your future. If you don't carve out some time for you and your plan, you will end up in this same spot next year, and the year after that. I'm not saying don't be involved; just use moderation. Perhaps in order to get your new part-time business off the ground, you have to have at least two nights a week free. Be honest but firm with the people whom you normally meet with on these nights; most of the time they will understand and be supportive. Don't assume that someone will think less of you because you are unavailable. Have you tried being unavailable? You might be surprised that they go on just fine without you, leaving you the necessary time to work on yourself and your own life.

Chapter Six
The Journey

Essential Tools

- Concentrate on creating multiple sources of income.

- The first person who must believe in an idea is you.

- The leverage of networking gives the opportunity to bring riches to your door.

- Visualize the person you wish to be and you will become that person.

- Becoming a person of quality requires careful thought, planning, and constant evaluation.

Journal/Notes

Chapter Seven

Begin with the End

10

Chapter Seven

Begin with the End

"Far better it is to dare mighty things, to win glorious triumphs, even though checkered by failure, than to take rank with those poor spirits who neither enjoy much nor suffer much, because they live in the grey twilight that knows not victory nor defeat."

– Theodore Roosevelt

I have spoken at and attended seminars that have been very successful in which the majority of attendees had a great experience. Unfortunately in such an audience, you will very often have a few people who destroy their own experience by becoming irritated because they had to wait in line a little too long to get food or coffee, or their name tag was misspelled. Personally, I made a choice many years ago that I would never let these complaints irritate or disappoint me. The best response I have found if you hear another person express such views is, "Isn't that interesting," and then move on to another subject. Focusing on minute issues that don't matter can distract you and interfere with potentially life-changing opportunities. In effect, you are accepting what that person is projecting, and it is very easy to echo that back in kind.

Having big goals is important. They will stretch you to grow, and quite possibly scare and excite you at the same time. When you constantly focus on your big goal, you will build a burning desire to achieve it. It will keep you focused and decrease the chance of these small, pitiful distractions throwing you off course.

Persistence

By definition, persistence is the ability to remain in an endeavor or action in spite of adverse conditions or occurrences. You have to ask yourself, "How many times can you be knocked down and still get up and keep going? What is your limit? When will you quit?" Have you given yourself a timeline in which you will try all this "goal" stuff, and if it doesn't work, go back to what you are doing? Have you given yourself a worst-case scenario that will excuse you from trying anymore? If so, then you are giving yourself a reason to fail. You are hedging your bets rather than giving it one-hundred percent and you know what? You're right; you will absolutely fail.

I know of a bestselling writer, Jodi Thomas, who tells the story of her career:

I was a school teacher and my husband is also a school teacher. We struggled to make ends meet with two young boys. I had always wanted to write a novel and so I decided to do it, hoping I could at least put some money away for the boys' college education. I finished my first book in about a year and sent it out to every publisher in New York. Just as quickly, they sent it right back. The rejections were harsh, and one even included a two page single-spaced letter from a leading editor about how bad it really was. It hurt terribly. Many times when I was depressed, I go out to Llano Cemetery and sit for a while. It is calm and serene and gives me space to think. On one particular day, I was walking among the beautiful landscape and happened to see a large granite fruit bowl in the distance. I walked over and saw this bowl was surrounded by benches, so I sat for a while and cried my eyes out, certain that every dream I had of being published had been washed away. Finally, I looked down and on the cement by my feet was the word "triumph."

I thought it strange that there would be a word in the cement and started looking around the bowl of fruit. Each side of the bowl had a different word making up a single sentence. That sentence was "Triumph Comes Through Perseverance." I decided right then that those publishers in New York may never like one word that I write, but I refuse to quit.

She sold her next book and now, twenty-eight years later, has published more than thirty novels and is a New York Times best-selling author.

This is a good illustration of the fact that you can't pick a stopping point before you start. You can't say, "I will try it for a year and then I'll let myself give up." You have to give it everything you have and determine in your own mind that there is no going back.

After high school I worked different jobs, did my military service, and when I applied to business school, a few people questioned if I would make it, saying I didn't have the right background in mathematics and economics. Some even advised me to first take an extra year in these subjects to give myself a better chance. I figured that if the school admitted me, they probably thought I could make it so why shouldn't I believe in myself as well? I thought extra studies would just delay me an extra year, so I decided instead to study extra on the side while doing the first year.

I struggled the first year and failed miserably in three subjects. Doubt set in, and some people probably thought they were justified in their predictions that I wouldn't make it. Encouragement from my parents and others close to me, together with a bit of the "winner's attitude" learned through my years in sports, got me through. When I finished, I even had additional experience from student organizational activities, had played soccer on a fairly high level and worked on vacations. I could have said "I will give it a year and try," but instead, I set a goal to finish among the top ten percent on the estimated four years with a particular grade point average. I missed the GPA goal by 1/100 of a point, but imagine how far I would have missed the mark if I'd allowed others' opinions to affect me.

> *If you do not give yourself the opportunity to quit, then you will be forced to move forward.*

I heard a story once about a general who sent his army across the sea to an island to do battle. When they landed, the general and his lieutenant climbed the hill and realized that the opposing forces where many times greater than their army. The lieutenant asked the general what they should do, expecting him to say, "Retreat." Instead the general said, "Burn the lifeboats."

In your own life, you must determine to burn your lifeboats. If you do not give yourself the opportunity to quit, then you will be forced to move forward.

Think about your purpose. Is it to provide a better life for your children or maybe give yourself time and monetary freedom? Many of you have probably seen or heard about people who survive incredible hardships: from accidents to days or weeks stranded on the open ocean. How do they do it? What separates them from the normal person that would die very quickly? The answer is that most of them have a very strong will to live. They have a strong purpose and a vision that they will overcome every hardship.

You create this with your own purpose and vision. While the stakes may not be life and death, they are your future and represent the life you want. When you come upon hard times or face what may seem to be insurmountable obstacles, focusing on your purpose will get you through and set you on the path to success again.

> *Embrace the changes in your life with a good attitude.*

Satisfaction

As you go through your plan, you will reach the goals you set one by one, and you will set new goals and strive toward them as well. If this is the process, you may wonder how to know when you've "made it." At what point do you take a deep breath and proclaim, "I've arrived!" This is different for every individual. Some have a set goal, amount of money, or a timeframe that they pursue; others leave it open-ended.

I know that you will reach a satisfied and fulfilling life much sooner than you realize, once you start on your own path to success. I mentioned earlier that some years ago I worked in a large company. I enjoyed work and the challenges that came with my responsibilities. However, after five years of sixty- to eighty-hour work weeks and traveling one hundred forty days a year, I felt as if something was missing in life. Although I was very satisfied with having a great job with a decent salary, I had come to a point where I was out of balance with other important areas in my life.

When I decided to make changes, I hesitated and went through all kinds of thoughts, doubts, and fears, but as many people experience in similar situations, once the decision was made and I started moving and taking actions toward my new goals, it was more a relief and the fears diminished. At the time of decision, I thought it would take me several years to "turn around" and achieve a more satisfying lifestyle. My experience, however, was that I felt immediately successful and within a few months I felt a freedom I had never felt before.

You see, few realize that success isn't a thing; it's an emotion. We feel successful; therefore we are. There are people who are perfectly content and happy working the job that they have, raising their children and spending time with family. There is no rule that says you have to be dissatisfied with these elements of your life to pursue your purpose. This is merely a starting point. You can always improve, but the path to success isn't about getting there. It's about the journey. Earl Nightingale once pointed out in *Lead the Field* that "Success is the progressive realization of a worthy ideal." What will you find out about yourself and others as you go? What lessons will you learn and want to share with those who may one day approach you and ask you to be their mentor?

Part of a successful attitude and lifestyle is the ability to give back to your community, to your family, and to others who seek to learn what you know. As you achieve greater heights, you may notice that the goals that you set have more to do with moving others forward rather than yourself. This is a natural result of living a lifestyle that is in harmony with your purpose and the universe. It becomes second nature to uplift others and help them find their way. You honor those who helped you by concentrating your efforts on those whom you can now help.

> *You create this with your own purpose and vision.*

I Have What It Takes

Repeat these words to yourself often. Type them up and hang them on your refrigerator, wall or computer. Look at them each day and believe in yourself.

Embrace the changes in your life with a good attitude. Convince yourself that you can and will do whatever it takes to meet your goals and live the life you dream of.

Be patient. Change doesn't happen overnight and this will take time. Another of the universal laws is the Law of Gender. This law states that every seed has a gestation or incubation period. Ideas are very much the same. They need time to germinate and grow within the mind to become fully formed.

For a physical seed, it is quite obvious; ask any gardener about the gestation period when putting a plant seed in the ground, and he can tell you with high accuracy when the plant or grass will arise. Similarly, when a woman becomes pregnant, a doctor would be able to tell her with a high level of certainty when the baby is to be expected. However, when it comes to a "mental" seed, for example, when you get an idea and set a goal, it becomes more difficult. We can guess at a time and a date when we want to reach a goal, but we would only be guessing. No one has ever figured out the incubation or gestation period of a mental seed to manifest in physical form.

I often jokingly say that, "I never missed a goal, but I seldom reached it on time, either." Nature abhors a vacuum, so don't give yourself too much time on your way to your goal. If you don't reach it on time, it's not because you failed to reach your goal; you just guessed wrong on the date, and the date is part of your plan. Keep the goal if it still feels worthy of you, and adjust the plan and the date which is part of that plan. Be aware that most of the time we don't reach a goal exactly on the time we guessed. Usually it takes a little longer or we reach it a little earlier. Don't get frustrated. It's just part of the game that the universal intelligence has constructed for us. If you don't reach it on time, give yourself a little more and move on. Remember that this is about the journey. No one gets to the top of the mountain in one day; you ascend step by step with dogged persistence.

Take time to appreciate who you are right now and who you want to become. Someday you will look back and be very proud of the decisions that you are making today and the changes you are implementing.

> *Take time to appreciate who you are right now and who you want to become.*

Learn to listen and think before you speak. A big part of learning is to be quiet and let others teach you. You will never know what you miss by talking. Others have valid input that can help you, and they want to help you. Let them.

Don't fear change or uncertainty. We usually are the most apprehensive about things that we don't have definite outcomes or solutions to. Believe that you have the ability to solve any problem that will arise and don't imagine monsters in the closet. Get the facts, do your homework, and boldly move forward. You mustn't let the risk of failure keep you from the glorious rewards that await you.

Chapter Seven
Begin with the End

Essential Tools

- Persistence is the ability to remain in an endeavor or action in spite of adverse conditions or circumstances.

- Don't pick a stopping point before you start.

- The satisfaction of success is the biggest reward.

- You have what it takes to be successful.

- Reaching your goals and achieving success is all about the journey.

Journal/Notes

Chapter Eight
The Slippery Slope of Habit

14

Chapter Eight

The Slippery Slope of Habit

The better a man is, the more mistakes he will make, for the more new things he will try. I would never promote to a top-level job a man who was not making mistakes... otherwise he is sure to be mediocre."

— Peter Drucker

One of the interesting phenomena of the human mind is that we long for the familiar comfort zone that we have become accustomed to. It makes no difference whether this comfort zone is good or bad; it is just familiar. This is why you see people who are constantly poor remain poor. They are choosing to project the same attitude they always have, and the universe has no choice but to echo that same attitude back to them. It doesn't matter if they work in a factory or are one of the top wage earners in their industry. They have always known the lack of money and will perpetuate that.

A while ago I read an article in the news that an astonishing high number of people who win large sums of money on lottery finds themselves having lost the money within a relatively short time. Some even find themselves in a worse financial situation than they were before they won the money. Their preconditioned ideas about money prevent them from handling it well.

You see the same force at work in relationships as well. Those who have been in abusive situations will tend to remain in them, and not because they necessarily want to. They just don't believe their lives can be different and have no faith in themselves to even try to make it so. You often see that women who get out of an abusive relationship soon after attract a similar person to be their new boyfriend, and once again find themselves in a similar situation.

The mind only knows what we have done in the past. When we provide it with information to suggest that we could do something significantly better, for instance, in terms of sales performance or personally doubling our income, it will reject that information because it does not fit in with our past experiences. We then feel discomfort in relation to the new idea. We reject the idea of doing better because of the associated discomfort.

Anytime you step out of your comfort zone, you will feel anxious and uncomfortable. You should welcome that feeling; it means you are growing as a person.

Bob Proctor refers to this as the Terror Barrier. Leaping out into unknown or into new territory is both exciting and frightening. It is this mixture of emotions that can confuse and distract. Your mind will create fear as you strive toward your goal and, if you let yourself dwell on that fear, it will manifest itself as reality.

My wife told me about the time when she was to hold her first sales presentation and how nervous she was. I spoke with a couple who were there, sitting on the first row and they felt so sorry for her, so much so they felt they "had to buy." Today she is one of the world leaders in her industry and a person for thousands of others to emulate and follow. She has spoken on stage at large events and conventions in many of the largest cities in Germany such as Berlin and Hamburg. She has done the same in Zurich, Helsinki, London, Copenhagen, Amsterdam, Oslo, Stockholm, Moscow and more, with audiences ranging from hundreds to thousands of people. I have done the same, and it is an awesome feeling once you know you master the ability to speak in front of others.

I can assure you no one is "born" with the skills to speak on stage, whether there are two or a thousand people listening. It is a learned skill. It requires a good deal of work and training, but I am convinced that anyone can do it if they really wanted to. You will also go through that excitement or "fear" every time you get ready to speak, but the rewards from delivering are so great that I would do it again and again.

You may have had the exhilaration and excitement of performing on stage at some point in your life. Even the most seasoned actor will feel anxious and uncertain before the curtain rises. It's almost as if the mind is giving a final warning before you step onto the stage. It is no different when you are striving toward big goals. The closer you get to achieving them, the more you are pulled back into the comfort zone you have always known.

It is sometimes as if some people are afraid of success. A friend of mine was close to achieving a big goal for a long time, but just almost got there. Looking back, when she finally made it she understood what had been holding her back from reaching that big goal was the fear of what would come with success. She had this picture in her mind of even greater expectations and responsibilities being put on her shoulders, and she wasn't sure she could handle it. She would have to hold speeches from stage in front of hundreds of people and be expected to take on several leadership responsibilities that she felt she was not qualified or prepared for.

This is why so many times you see someone reach glorifying heights, then come crashing down in a fit of despair. You must believe in the power of your mind to focus on what you desire. You must also be aware of the power that your past has over your thoughts when you are trying to bring change into your life.

There is a big difference between knowing and believing. Belief is an expression of faith. If we had perfect knowledge, we wouldn't need faith. When you really and truly **know** something will happen, there is no trace of doubt, no lingering thread of skepticism. Knowing travels beyond what would seem to be rational reality.

The "knowing" portion of our mind is the subconscious. You can think of it as a habit or idea that is fixed in place and nothing can shake that idea, even if it proves to be a completely irrational idea.

Anything which represents change to this "knowing" portion of our mind disrupts these habits and makes us uncomfortable. The new purpose, vision, and goals that you have set will cause major discomfort, but if you really desire to achieve the life you want, you will focus on them.

It is at this point that the conscious mind makes the decision to accept the new ideas. All that you have known and experienced rebels against this new idea, and before you know it fear sets in.

> *The new purpose, vision, and goals that you have set will cause major discomfort.*

When fear enters the picture, logic is abandoned. By concentrating on that fear, you attract more uncertainty and anxiety to yourself, and your goals seem even farther away. This is the point where many people can give up. Doubts can overwhelm and the subconscious begs for retreat back into what you have known, back into your comfort zone.

When I came straight out of business school and started working with IBM in sales, I had high ambitions. I remember when first meeting with experienced customers, I felt they knew so much and I so little about the technologies I was selling. Fear of not succeeding, of not being good enough, sneaked into my mind. Logic would say that most other sales representatives must have been in similar situations when they were new, and if they came through it, so would I. Good colleagues and experienced managers encouraged me and helped me get over that phase. Left alone, I would probably have given it up. I believe many talented people got lost in different companies without that necessary support and give up a possibly great career due to being conquered by fear and having no one there to help alleviate those fears. It was fortunate that IBM was the kind of company that took good care of me and directed me through those first difficult times.

You know now that by concentrating on the positive goal ahead and setting those fears aside that you are imprinting new ideas into your subconscious. If you do this enough and concentrate on the changes you want to make and the goals you are trying to achieve, you are allowing the new ideas to win. You are empowering your mind with new thoughts, which result in different actions.

One of the problems that people have is trying to figure out all the details of how big goals are going to be met. They lose sight of the fact that until a mindset conducive to meeting them has been created, they don't have a chance. You start a career and want to become president of the company one day. Until you have made the decision to go after that position, you will probably not find out how to get there.

> *You set the goal, map out the road, and approximate a time when you will get there. Then you aim at the first goal.*

The same is true when you head out of the harbor with your boat for the next distance, when you drive the car out of the garage to go on a trip, when you are going on vacation, or if you are starting a new business. You will never find solutions on how to arrive there unless you have made the decision to go there first. Make the decision, take the first step in the direction of your goal, and then you can adjust to the new circumstances to take the next step. Consider going with the car from Oslo to Copenhagen. You couldn't possibly know before starting exactly how you are going to get there, every road work, accident or detour that would slow you down. You deal with that when you get to it. You set the goal, map out the road, and approximate a time when you will get there. Then you aim at the first goal.

The Stages of Change

It is important to understand that people go through specific stages in their attempt to cope with change. Understanding that this is a normal progression helps avoid overreacting to resistance. These stages have been described much like the stages of grief. This is very fitting as the subconscious is being forced to let go of old habits; in effect, it slowly kills them off and the mind must adjust to new ideas.

Stage I: Denial

An early strategy that people use to cope with change is to deny the necessity for them. They often view new ideas as suitable for others, but hope it isn't necessary for them.

People in the denial stage are trying to avoid dealing with the fear and uncertainty of prospective change. They are hoping they won't have to adapt.

It's hardly news to anyone today that the world is changing. A company going about their business exactly the same way today as they did five years ago is probably on their way out of business. If you were to study the Fortune 500's list of the biggest companies ten to twenty years ago and compare with the similar list today, you would find that most of them are not on the map anymore.

Today's top executives in corporations follow the changes, know what's going on, and adjust accordingly, or they are very soon without a job. Employees should do the same. Within almost any profession, unless you really pay attention, you could surprisingly find yourself obsolete and on the market for another job.

As I am writing this, I am in Germany. I just got off the phone with a nice lady at customer service in Norwegian Airlines. In perfect Norwegian language and with an accent similar to my own, she gave me quick and accurate service and rebooked my ticket at a minor fee. Nothing special with that, you may think; it was also what I expected. What was special with this experience was that this nice lady was a local sitting in Riga. This young, bright woman works in a call centre set up by a Norwegian friend of mine. He is building a great business in the Baltic countries offering Norwegian Airlines and other companies possibilities to offer their customers (me, in his case) excellent service at a low cost and with high quality. They provide this at a fraction of the cost compared to what it would cost these companies to deliver the same service from a call centre in Norway.

Another friend of ours travels to the Baltic countries a couple of times a month and teaches these young people how to perfect their Norwegian language skills that they learned in university. I happen to know this, but as a regular customer, I would just call a Norwegian phone number and believe that the person I spoke with was sitting somewhere in Norway. Today, a company can chose a cost-effective service from almost anywhere in the world. Technology has brought us closer and the world is getting smaller every day. Many executives in corporations know this and adjust to it to keep cost low, service high, and be competitive in the market place. The question is, are you as an employee, or as a business leader, adjusting? Are you preparing yourself for this future or are you in denial? As Bill Gates so beautifully put it, "One thing is clear: we don't have the option of turning away from the future. No one gets to vote on whether technology is going to change our lives." Those who hope they won't need to adapt as a part of a corporation or as an individual will soon be out of business and without a job. The sad thing is that "crisis" often needs to hit before many recognize it.

> *People tend to move out of the denial stage when they see solid, tangible indicators that things are different.*

The denial stage is difficult because it is hard to involve people in planning for the future when they will not acknowledge that the future is going to be any different than the present.

People tend to move out of the denial stage when they see solid, tangible indicators that things *are* different. Even with these indicators, some people can remain in denial for some time.

Stage II: Anger and Resistance

When people can no longer deny that something must change, they tend to move into a state of anger, accompanied by covert resistance. As a corporate executive, I worked in the travel industry through some of the toughest years of change in history for travel agencies. We had to make several unpopular but necessary decisions that impacted the employees of the company. At one point, we were told by the chairman and the board to take a major cost reduction, which meant letting ten percent of all employees in the company go. Many middle managers and employees saw this was coming due to major changes in the industry, but since we had one of our best years in history, they went through denial. Faced with the fact of layoffs, that denial turned into anger and frustration as many couldn't believe this would happen to them, especially as we had such good results. Unions were engaged in negotiations, and even some "fights" occurred.

This stage is the most critical with respect to the success of the new ideas. A mentor or guide is often needed to help work through the anger and to move people to the next stage. If guidance is poor, the anger at this stage may last indefinitely, perhaps much longer than even the memory of the change itself. Who knows, there may even be people today who are still angry at the company and the executives (us) for what had to be done during those times. We knew that if we hadn't done what was needed, we would have risked the whole company's existence, and everybody's job would be in danger down the road.

Stage III: Exploration and Acceptance

This is the stage where people see the positive effect of implementing the changes in their lives. They have stopped denying, and while they still may be somewhat uncomfortable, the anger has moved out of the spotlight. They have a better understanding of the meaning of the change, and are more willing to explore further and to accept the change. They act more open-mindedly and are now more interested in planning for their future and expecting more change.

Stage IV: Commitment

This is the payoff stage where people commit to the changes and are willing to work toward making it succeed. They know it is a reality, and at this point people have adapted sufficiently to succeed.

The change process takes a considerable amount of time to stabilize and to work. Don't underestimate the power of old habits by assuming they will "work themselves out" and don't overreact when faced with reasonable resistance.

A Setback is not Defeat

Few who choose a new path for their lives get everything right the first time. Often there will be setbacks, but you must not let setbacks, or the fear of setbacks, keep you from achieving your goals. One of the most challenging aspects of a setback is the speed at which you recover and regain your direction and momentum. If you recover quickly, you will be back on track in short order, but often this is the point where your subconscious will try to convince you that you should step back and take some time to "get yourself together." This is a dangerous mindset, and one which can lead you right back into your old comfort zone.

Remember Newton's law. "An object at rest stays at rest while an object in motion stays in motion." The longer you wait around to "recover," the harder it will be to move forward. By the time you try, will be very much like starting completely over.

A friend of mine got fired from a position as divisional sales manager. When I told him that it could be the best that ever happened to him, he took months to go through all four stages: denial, anger and retaliation, and finally acceptance of the situation and commitment to change. Today, he is a successful business entrepreneur with several businesses and makes more in a month than he did in a year before he was fired. However, he waited a long time to get back on track, which you could say cost him millions, compared to if he had accepted the situation, taken responsibility for it and committed to change right away. The slippery slope of old habits will try to steal your dream.

One of the reasons that I talk at length about the ideas of personal responsibility and accountability in Chapter Five is for you to understand that it is your choice how you will deal with setbacks. Setbacks become failures only when you refuse to believe that you have control. You can always decide to respond in a calm and confident way rather than react to the situation. Animals and people with low levels of awareness react. It is "fight or flight" for them, whereas a person with the understanding and awareness will respond in a calm manner.

You always have control over your reactions. If your reaction to a setback is to quit, then you have truly failed. However, if you grasp the knowledge that you have the power to change and that no failure, no matter how devastating, can stop you, then you have gained ultimate freedom.

Inertia, like gravity, is a powerful force. Even when current habits are frustrating, annoying or time wasting, their familiarity and predictability make them difficult to put aside. Some would say that the idea of tapping into the universal laws in regard to your personal or business life is an outlandish idea. I can tell you from experience; it is the only way to achieve what you desire. No one ever achieved great things that didn't imagine an outlandish goal in their minds first. They felt it, dreamed it, and then created that reality. That reality can be yours as well.

> *You can always decide to respond in a calm and confident way rather than react to the situation.*

Chapter Eight

The Slippery Slope of Habit

Essential Tools

- Recognize that we long for our own comfort zone.

- Anytime you step out of your comfort zone, you will feel anxious and uncomfortable.

- Fear of success holds many people back.

- Recognize the stages of change and welcome them.

- Understand a setback is not a defeat.

Journal/Notes

Chapter Nine

The Wealthiest Person in the World

$13\frac{1}{2}$

Chapter Nine

The Wealthiest Person in the World

"Despite what we've been taught, we don't have to be rich, famous or distinguished to make our dreams come true."

– Sharon Cook and Graciela Sholander

Everything you accomplish begins with your decision. Bob Proctor defines a decision as "a single mental move you can make which, in a millisecond, will solve enormous problems for you. It has the potential to improve almost any personal or business situation you will ever encounter . . . and it could literally propel you down the path to incredible success." He goes on to say that not only your income, but your whole life is dominated by the power of your decisions. "The health of your mind and body, the well-being of your family, your social life, and the type of relationships you develop" are a direct reflection of the sound decisions you make.

The decision to change your life and your mindset begins with that first step. Both in my personal and business experience, I have learned that decision- making is a skill that none of us are taught. It isn't part of the curriculum of our university business colleges. Effective decision making means that you can *make things happen* instead of just *letting* things happen. Decision making is active and required in every aspect of life. It is involved in a variety of situations and problems, from the very simple to the very complex. Making decisions which direct and guide events and actions of life into a planned course, rather than letting events fall to chance, is the key to following your dreams.

Developing the Art of Decision Making

Everyone, young or old, can learn to improve their decision making skills. Making a decision is not something you do from habit; decision making requires conscious thought. Life consists of a series of decisions, and inaction is just as much a choice as action. Every decision we make is different from all others because we have had one more experience. Most decisions are made in a series; you do something and then do something else. Often, making one decision does not settle anything. Instead, it moves you into a position to make another decision. This can work for you or against you. If you are traveling along a path of good decisions, then they build upon one another to create a great life. If you make a series of bad decisions, your life can quickly spiral out of control.

Being a good decision maker and making clear decisions also makes you attractive. In personal relationships, most men and women find a person of the opposite sex more attractive as a partner if they "know where they're going in life."

If you take on leadership in any organization - business or other type - and want people to follow you, you better make clear decisions on where you are going. Why would anyone ever follow you if they don't have an idea of where they will end up? A network marketing professional was "stuck" and came to me one day to ask if I could help finding what's wrong. After being rather successful for a while, this person seemed to have "lost the magic," and had gone from being a good recruiter to not being able to attract the right people anymore. I asked what her goal was and she looked down. She had lost focus and was not attractive. I remember what a leading business executive once said when asked about the three most important critical factors for success. His answer was, "Recruit, recruit, and recruit!" It is as true for any business, whether it is based on network marketing or traditional marketing and sales. A business that is not attractive for new people will sooner or later go out of business. It is only a matter of time. You grow or die.

A human resources manager in a Scandinavian consultant firm told me a while ago that their number one critical success factor is that in order to maintain and grow their position in the market place, they have to be attractive enough to *recruit* at minimum two hundred of the best students from the best universities and business schools in the country every year. She succeeds, so she is apparently really good at what she does.

The Decision Making Process

Consider the goal or goals you want to reach. The goals you choose are influenced by your purpose and vision. Solidifying that purpose and vision allows you to prioritize your goals.

A method that has helped me a lot in decision making as well as in teaching others to become more independent and empowered in their work situation was given by Dale Carnegie in his book *How to Stop Worrying and Start Living*. Whenever I am in a situation where I need to make a decision, I ask myself these four questions. If they are bigger decisions, I write the answers down on a piece of paper because writing makes it all clearer. In addition to the four questions, I have added two other action points that I have found useful:

- What is the problem?

- What caused the problem?

- What possible solutions to the problem can you see?

- What solution do you suggest? What is your decision?

- Take action and assume responsibility.

- Evaluate your results and learn from them.

The steps in making and implementing decisions as they apply to changing your life are as follows:

1. What is the problem? Recognize the problem and write it down.

The decision making process starts by recognizing that a problem exists. Something has to be changed in the situation, and there are possibilities for improvement. Big problems must often be broken down into smaller, more manageable goals while focusing on your ultimate purpose. Carnegie used the example of the problem of an insurance salesperson called Frank Bettger. Frank had lost his enthusiasm, started doubting himself, and was ready to quit. He was not able to produce the sales results he wanted, despite having numerous customer meetings.

2. Analyze the problem. What caused the problem?

Once the problem is identified, study it carefully to find exactly what is causing it. Dissatisfaction and disillusionment are some of the biggest reasons that people choose a better life. Frank Bettger started analyzing the problem and found a pattern in his sales reports for the last twelve months: Seventy percent of the sales had happened in the first meeting, twenty-three percent in meeting number two, and only seven percent of the sales occurred from meeting the same customer the third, fourth or fifth time. This meant he used fifty percent of his working hours on the part of his business that produced only seven percent of the sales.

3. Look for opportunities. What are the possible solutions?

In Frank's case, there was one obvious solution. In this case, you may try to look from different perspectives and see if there is more than one possible solution to your problem. Think and look for as many opportunities as possible. In most situations, if you are open to receiving new thoughts and ideas, opportunities will find you.

Analyze each opportunity in relation to your overall purpose and see if it is a good fit. If so, proceed, but if not, reject it. It is not about taking every opportunity that comes your way, but about choosing the right opportunities.

4. What solution do you suggest?

Frank Bettger's answer was obvious. He would cut all customer visits after visit number two and used some time to work out new plans. The results were incredible. In a short period of time, he doubled the average value of every single meeting. He went on to become one of the most famous insurance salespeople of his time in the USA. The question is, can you use these questions on your business problems, family or relationships

problems? I personally use them on any problem or challenge I
am up against in all areas of life. Can you use this to reduce your
worries by fifty percent as Frank did?

Having a so-called "open door policy" that was so
popular for a while, I was often interrupted by employees that
had problems they wanted me to help them with. By asking all
employees to use this method and write down the answers on
a piece of paper before they came to me, I eliminated at least
seventy-five percent of the visits. By the time they had written
down the answers, the decision was obvious in most cases, and
they didn't have to involve me.

5. Put your decision into action and accept the responsibility.

You, too, must put your decision into action. Making a
decision and then not acting upon it relegates the decision to a
wish or hope. Action is absolutely required to reap any benefits
or see any positive feedback. Remember, go with what you have.
Progress before perfection!

After you make a decision, you need to accept the
responsibility and consequences. You need to be willing to live
with that decision, or else make another decision to change
direction. Most decisions are made without having all the
information you'd like and all the resources you really need. Don't
be afraid to make a decision just because you may have to revise it.
That's part of the process.

6. Evaluate your results and learn from them.

The outcome, or result of your decisions, should be evaluated regularly to determine their effectiveness. Frank Bettger's reports helped him analyze the problem when he got stuck. Continuously ask yourself three questions: What am I doing? What's working? What isn't?

Resist Limitations

Once we decide to do something, conditions change. The resources that you need to fulfill your vision will come to you. You'll always find what you need if that's your focus. I know that some of you may think this concept is absurd. However, I personally have experience with it in my business and want to help you apply it in yours. Do you want to be focused on your limitations or your opportunities for success?

One of the things we often let get in our way are what people call circumstances. How many times do circumstances stand between you and what you want to accomplish? Don't use circumstances as an excuse to keep you from being responsible for your decisions!

Napoleon said, "Circumstances, I make them." My point is that we can examine how you make decisions and view circumstance. Your viewpoint can change, if needed. It's up to you. Just make the decision and then take the next step.

We talked earlier about the fear of failure or setbacks. If you fail at something, it doesn't make you a failure. However, if you decide to quit, it is a conscious act of your own.

> *Just make the decision and then take the next step.*

Thomas Edison didn't have a working light bulb the first time he attempted it, but he kept on working. His decision was to succeed, and his focus was to keep at it until he did. Most people don't know that he had 10,000 failures before he succeeded in making a light bulb that actually worked. Like Edison, as long as you keep your mind on your ultimate purpose and persevere, you will succeed.

Most of us understand that fear is a natural emotion that protects us from danger. However, fear can also be a motivator. The problem with stepping outside of our comfort zone is that people imagine danger that doesn't actually exist. They confuse fear with risk, which can be paralyzing.

Allowing yourself to get caught up in fear can keep you from making the right decision at the right time. Old fears from our past can be projected onto a new situation that you haven't experienced before. Negative emotion and energy gets stronger with this type of mindset.

Paralyzing Perfection

Do you remember what I told you when I started a business? I had the bag full of plans, calculations and spreadsheets on how to develop the business and got very good advice from my friend and mentor Wolfgang Sonnenburg: Progress before perfection. Go with what you have. Until it is up and running, don't use too much time on the "how." Too many treat their life and their business as if they want to go from Oslo to Copenhagen by car and never get out of the drive way; they're still sitting in the garage planning the details of the trip! The risk is you will get there too late or more likely, never at all!

You may hear some people talk about perfectionism as though it is a good thing, but it is actually an extreme form of fear. Perfectionism sets up fear of failure before you even start a task because you constantly think that everything you do has to be perfect, so you never do anything at all. You may do a lot of planning and thinking, but you never seem to move forward. If you are setting an objective that your life will be perfect and that every decision must be perfect, then it is a guarantee that you will be disappointed.

One of the main sources of this perfectionism is fear of criticism. In addition to the criticism that people often feel that they receive from others, they also have to deal with the incredibly powerful inner critic. This critic is particularly damaging, killing off ideas before they even get properly formed. I'm sure that everybody will be able to recognize the pattern of thought where when an idea comes up to stretch the comfort zone, so all of the reasons why it is a "bad idea" rapidly spring forth in the mind.

The answer is to swap perfection for excellence both in your personal and professional life. The dictionary defines excellence as relating to any activity in which one is outstanding, but I prefer another definition used by Bob Proctor. He says that it means having a commitment to completion. Such commitment comes about as a result of making a definite decision to do something.

All of us experience our own fear or terror barrier, whether that comes in the form of perfectionism or an inability to see our lives any differently than they currently are. The secret to living a life of abundance is to be able to imagine abundance in your mind and hold the image until old habits and paradigms melt away. Success is as much a habit as failure can be, and it is your choice whether or not you will choose it.

This book is the culmination and manifestation of a dream I have held in my own mind. I want to encourage you to take these ideas and design your life, your career, or your business the way you want it. Although you may have certain family obligations to consider and honor, I believe that you can advance far in determining the life you want.

> *Success is as much a habit as failure can be, and it is your choice whether or not you will choose it.*

These ideas have helped me and thousands, if not millions, of others to provide the life they want. I have experienced everything from improved personal relationships to tripling my business results in a few months. I know huge corporations have increased their sales with hundreds of millions of dollars in a relatively short time when using these ideas the correct way. I have seen teenagers go from shy individuals with low self-esteem and poor results in school into becoming top "A" students when coached on these ideas. I believe you can take charge and improve the results in your life dramatically, as well as the results in your business, no matter what your present circumstances are or what your background is.

If you are already living a good life, that doesn't mean it can't be better. You can always be, do, and have more. As a matter of fact, striving to continuously improve your life in different areas is essential. As I have pointed out, you either go forward in life, or you are going backward. You are either projecting positive energy and receiving that positive life echo, or you are receiving negativity. Have you ever met a one-hundred meter runner who didn't want to run faster? How often do you meet a worker who doesn't want to earn more, or a sportsman or woman who doesn't want to improve their results? Absolutely nothing stands still. You may hear some people say, "I like it just the way it is." They are just advertising their ignorance (lack of knowledge) of this specific law. If that's your decision and your thinking, to "like and keep it just the way it is," then you are in for a disappointment. That I guarantee you, just as sure as the sun sets tonight in Oslo.

> *If you are already living a good life, that doesn't mean it can't be better. You can always be, do and have more.*

Make a decision to advance and to grow in life and in your career or business. If you would like us to help you, you will find our contact details in the back of this book. It is "on purpose" for us to help others increase their understanding and become aware of these magnificent ideas that can help them and their businesses design the lives, creating the lifestyle and results of their dreams.

Your life as it is right now is merely the manifestation of how you were programmed to think. You can choose to think differently. You can choose to "think abundantly" in every facet of your life and create a life, a career, or a business beyond your wildest dreams.

This is by no means "the end" for me. I am still on a marvellous journey of life, seeking to improve every day while making sure that I enjoy each step of the way. I wish the same for you and wish you a life of abundance in all areas!

Chapter Nine
The Wealthiest Person in the World

Essential Tools

- Anything you will ever accomplish begins with a decision.

- Constantly work to improve your decision making skills.

- Know where you are going in life.

- Recognize the problems that exist and analyze them.

- Look for as many opportunities as possible.

- Go with what you have. Progress before perfection!

- Resist any and all limitations.

Journal/Notes

References

Bob Proctor, *You Were Born Rich*

Raymond Holiwell, *Working with the Law*

Earl Nightingale and Bob Proctor, *The New Lead The Field*

Napoleon Hill, *Think and Grow Rich*

OTHER BOOKS FROM LifeSuccess Publishing

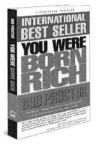

You Were Born Rich

Bob Proctor
ISBN # 978-0-9656264-1-5

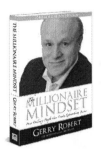

The Millionaire Mindset
*How Ordinary People Can
Create Extraordinary Income*

Gerry Robert
ISBN # 978-1-59930-030-6

Rekindle The Magic In
Your Relationship
Making Love Work

Anita Jackson
ISBN # 978-1-59930-041-2

Finding The Bloom of
The Cactus Generation
*Improving the quality of
life for Seniors*

Maggie Walters
ISBN # 978-1-59930-011-5

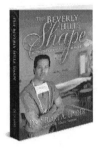

The Beverly Hills Shape
The Truth About Plastic Surgery

Dr. Stuart Linder
ISBN # 978-1-59930-049-8

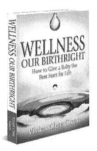

Wellness Our Birthright
*How to give a baby the best
start in life.*

Vivien Clere Green
ISBN # 978-1-59930-020-7

Lighten Your Load

Peter Field
ISBN # 978-1-59930-000-9

Change & How To
Survive In The New
Economy
*7 steps to finding freedom
& escaping the rat race*

Barrie Day
ISBN # 978-1-59930-015-3

OTHER BOOKS FROM LifeSuccess Publishing

Stop Singing The Blues
10 Powerful Strategies For
Hitting The High Notes In
Your Life

Dr. Cynthia Barnett
ISBN # 978-1-59930-022-1

Don't Be A Victim,
Protect Yourself
Everything Seniors Need To
Know To Avoid Being Taken
Financially

Jean Ann Dorrell
ISBN # 978-1-59930-024-5

A "Hand Up", not a
"Hand Out"
The best ways to help others
help themselves

David Butler
ISBN # 978-1-59930-071-9

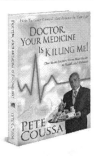

Doctor Your Medicine Is
Killing Me!
One Mans Journey From
Near Death to Health and
Wellness

Pete Coussa
ISBN # 978-1-59930-047-4

I Believe in Me
7 Ways for Woman to Step
Ahead in Confidence

Lisa Gorman
ISBN # 978-1-59930-069-6

The Color of Success
Why Color Matters in your
Life, your Love, your Lexus

Mary Ellen Lapp
ISBN # 978-1-59930-078-8

If Not Now, When?
What's Your Dream?

Cindy Nielsen
ISBN # 978-1-59930-073-3

The Skills to Pay the
Bills… and then some!
How to inspire everyone in
your organisation into high
performance!

Buki Mosaku
ISBN # 978-1-59930-058-0

OTHER BOOKS FROM LIFESUCCESS PUBLISHING

The Secret To Cracking
The Property Code
*7 Timeless Principles for
Successful Real Estate
Investment*

Richard S.G. Poole
ISBN # 978-1-59930-063-4

Why My Mother Didn't
Want Me To Be Psychic
*The Intelligent Guide To The
Sixth Sense*

Heidi Sawyer
ISBN # 978-1-59930-052-8

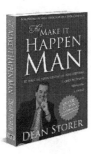

The Make It Happen Man
*10 ways to turn obstacles
into stepping stones without
breaking a sweat*

Dean Storer
ISBN # 978-1-59930-077-1

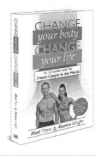

Change your body
Change your life
*with the Fittest Couple in
the World*

Matt Thom &
Monica Wright
ISBN # 978-1-59930-065-8

Good Vibrations!
*Can you tune in to a more
positive life?*

Clare Tonkin
ISBN # 978-1-59930-064-1

The Millionaire Genius
*How to wake up the money
magic within you.*

David Ogunnaike
ISBN # 978-1-59930-026-9

Scoring Eagles
*Improve Your Score In Golf,
Business and Life*

Max Carbone
ISBN # 978-1-59930-045-0

The Einstein Complex
*Awaken your inner genius,
live your dream.*

Dr. Roger A. Boger
ISBN # 978-1-59930-055-9

OTHER BOOKS FROM LifeSuccess Publishing

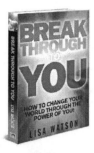

Break Through to You
How to Change Your World
Through the Power of You!

Lisa Watson
ISBN # 978-1-59930-084-9

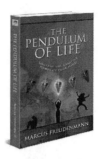

The Pendulum of Life
Unleash the Creative Power
of Your Mind

Marcus Freudenmann
ISBN # 978-1-59930-075-7

The Sweet Smell of Success
Health & Wealth Secrets

James "Tad" Geiger M.D.
ISBN # 978-1-59930-088-7

Living the Law of
Attraction
Real Stories of People
Manifesting Wealth,
Health and Happiness

Rich German, Andy Wong
& Robin Hoch
ISBN # 978-1-59930-091-7

Wealth Matters
Abundance is Your Birthlight

Chris J. Snook with
Chet Snook
ISBN # 978-1-59930-096-2

The Success Toolbox
For Entrepreneurs

Janis Vos
ISBN # 978-1-59930-005-4

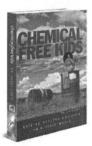

Chemical Free Kids
Raising Healthy Children in
a Toxic World

Dr. Sarah Lantz
ISBN # 978-1-59930-072-6

The Girlz Guide to
Building Wealth
...and men like it too

Maya Galletta, Aaron
Cohen, Polly McCormick,
Mike McCormick
ISBN # 978-1-59930-048-1